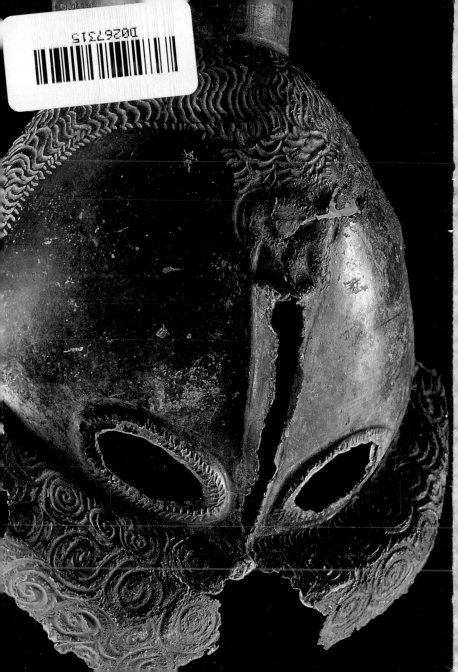

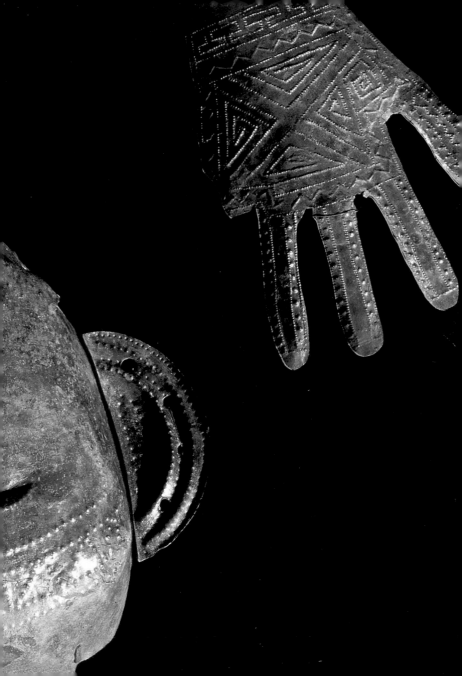

CONTENTS

THE CELTS
FIRST MASTERS OF EUROPE

Christiane Eluère

THAMES AND HUDSON

SEPVLTVRE
DE LA MOTTE S VALENTIN
COVRCELLES EN MONTAGNE, HTE MARNE
DECOVVERTE PAR HENRI MILLON
XIX IVIN MDCCCLXXX

At the close of the Bronze Age, in the turmoil at the dawn of history, horsemen armed with long swords, ancestors of the Celts, devised a new form of power. Between 900 and 600 BC, from Hallstatt to La Tène, a civilization emerged. It mastered iron, from which weapons of such value were forged that its warriors bore them even to the grave.

CHAPTER 1

BIRTH OF A WARRIOR ARISTOCRACY

Celtic princely graves abounded in tokens of refinement and wealth such as the Etruscan stamnos and Attic cantharos (left) from the barrow of La Motte-St-Valentin (Haute-Marne), or the odd little bronze bust (right) from Hallstatt (Austria) with its breastplate and arm rings.

In 1771 a cauldron containing 30 kg of gold coins and a golden torque came to light at Podmokly in Bohemia, and attracted the attention of scholars. While the whole of pre-Romantic Europe enthused about the legend of Ossian, a 3rd-century AD Gaelic bard rediscovered by the poet James Macpherson (1736–96), it was through the study of coinage that a disciplined revival of interest in the Celts began during the 18th century.

As archaeology developed during the 19th century, it became the chief source of knowledge about the Celts, and revealed a shared past that linked together different regions of Europe from the British Isles to the Carpathians. From then on, the ancient texts, numerous and explicit though they were, took second place to the sheer abundance of archaeological evidence.

The cauldron from Podmokly (above), shown amidst a few coins from the hoard in an engraving made in the year of its discovery (1771). It is encircled by the great torque, a twisted metal collar typically worn by Celtic warriors and deities.

19th-century archaeologists at work

As early as 1824 there were the first signs of the existence of an important Iron-Age cemetery at Hallstatt in Upper Austria; ancient salt mines had already been found there in the 14th century. Then, in 1857, excavations near Lake Neuchâtel, in Switzerland, led to the discovery at La Tène of masses of arms and personal ornaments. Hallstatt and La Tène

Among the first discoveries of Celtic archaeology was a sandstone cult pillar (left) from Pfalzfeld (Rhineland), found in 1608. It was originally topped by a head and would then have stood about 2.50 m high. Unprotected until 1934, it now measures only 1.48 m. It dates from 450 to 350 BC and probably stood on a barrow.

Hallstatt, in Upper Austria, is a small, completely isolated site in the heart of the Salzkammergut massif (left), accessible only by river. The climate is harsh, with little sunlight. Yet the site was very busy from the 7th to 5th centuries BC, probably on account of its salt mines. It combined all the right conditions for a new civilization to emerge and its remains to be preserved, and 2000 graves have been excavated in its astonishing early Celtic cemetery.

became eponymous sites whose names were used to denote the Early and Late Iron Age respectively.

At the end of the century many somehow related grave mounds were explored in southern Germany, Switzerland and eastern France. Meanwhile, the German archaeologist Heinrich Schliemann (1822–90) had discovered in 1874 in his search for the world of Homer the treasures of Mycenae and five of the six shaft-graves arranged in a circle. To the south-east of Rome, at Praeneste, the rich Etruscan Bernardini tomb had come to light. The concept of 'princely' protohistoric tombs and that of parallel development among Iron-Age societies, whether in Italy or in central Europe, then took a strong hold.

La Tène, located on a former branch of the River Thielle by the side of Lake Neuchâtel (Switzerland), was once an important crossing-place. In 1857 an antiques enthusiast, Hansli Kopp, found some very odd iron weapons there. The exceptional quantity of weapons recovered since then has justified archaeologists in regarding it as a representative site for the period of the greatest Celtic expansion. Battlefield, market or sanctuary – successive excavation campaigns have failed to determine the exact function of this Late Iron-Age centre.

Contemporary investigation

Excavation of Celtic burials continued during the 20th century, and went on producing sensational finds. The opening of the tomb at Vix (Côte-d'Or) in 1953, with its enormous bronze Greek krater, was a major event in world archaeology. In 1978, a barrow at Hochdorf, near Stuttgart, minutely excavated and then studied in the laboratory, yielded valuable information about its occupant's standard of living.

A new wave of excavations shed light upon settlements: the Heuneburg, a fortified site on the west bank of the Danube, the oppidum (fortified town) of Manching in Bavaria and Mont Beuvray (Nièvre). Sanctuaries were studied, such as Entremont and Roquepertuse in the South of France, Gournay-sur-Aronde (Oise), Fellbach-Schmiden in Württemberg and Snettisham in Norfolk.

Laboratory investigations made their own contribution through dendrochronology (a method of dating wood by observing tree growth rings) and the study of textiles, metals and organic substances – both macro- and micro-remains.

Protohistory and the 'Urnfields'

The Bronze and Iron Ages make up what is also known as protohistory, a period contemporary with

Early Iron-Age barrow topped by a sandstone statue at Kilchberg (Baden-Württemberg).

classical antiquity. These names, convenient because they refer to the technical evolution of the societies in question, were bestowed during the 19th century. At that time a sharp break between the two was believed to have occurred. Nowadays it is thought that the transition – in about the 8th century BC in western Europe – took place gradually, with a wide range of minor variations among different communities.

Similarly, the famous 'Urnfield' theory (so called from typical cremation cemeteries), which held that the proto-Celts were invaders from the east between the 13th and 8th centuries BC, has now been abandoned. Without necessarily insisting upon an exclusive line of descent from the Neolithic, it is now agreed that the Celts did evolve from populations already resident in Europe during the Bronze Age. In the 13th and 12th centuries BC we find that a few late Bronze-Age graves already prefigure the spectacular burial rites of the first Celtic princes. In the 11th century BC bronze parade equipment appeared that was clearly intended for votive offerings: breastplates from Fillinges (Savoie) and Marmesse (Haute-Marne), as well as wheels, shields and helmets in many other areas of Europe.

The close of the Bronze Age

At a crucial turning-point between the 9th and 8th centuries BC, the villages of temperate Europe often show a clear preoccupation with defence. Some put up

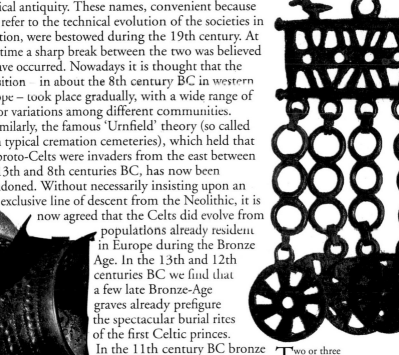

Two or three centuries before the epoch of the princes, symbols of prestige were already appearing that heralded the splendour of the 6th century BC: (opposite) the four-wheeled cart on a funerary urn from Sublaines (Indre-et-Loire), or (left) parade breastplates ritually deposited at Marmesse (Haute-Marne). The large pectoral (above) from a forest in the Jura, with a bird and wheels, combines traditional Bronze-Age motifs with Celtic exuberance.

palisades, like Choisy-au-Bac (Oise), or erected ramparts, like Hohlandsberg (Haut-Rhin). Villages on the shores of the French and Swiss lakes, that had prospered until then, disappeared within the space of a few years around 850 BC, and there is evidence to suggest deliberate arson. The feeling of insecurity is also reflected by a sudden increase in dwellings in caves at relatively high altitudes.

At the same time the climate deteriorated: it became colder and wetter, a trend that was to continue and intensify until the 6th century BC. Trade networks thinned out for unknown reasons and manufacturing activity was affected. Production of gold objects, previously so plentiful, began to tail off. Bronze goods were carefully salvaged by metallurgists or community officials, who buried them in hoards. Whether economic or social, there was certainly a crisis.

A small bronze figurine adorns a ritual axe from Hallstatt, Austria (below and left). Horsemen and cattle were favoured decorative themes during the 7th century BC in this dynamic area of central Europe, which was at a crossroads for influences from different sides of the Alps.

The new caste of horsemen

It was at this point that the first signs of a previously unknown order appeared: that of horsemen armed with long swords. They turn up sporadically, in ritual contexts and accompanied by goods such as a drinking-set, exotic imported items, a wagon burial and gold – all of which already foreshadow the

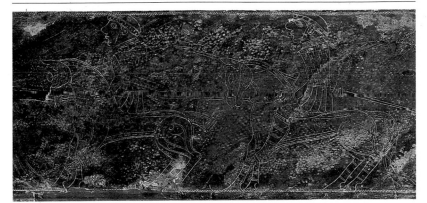

symbols of the new ruling class. Horse-riding was one of the innovations that marked out the powerful. In the cemetery at Chavéria (Jura), some twenty barrows have been excavated. Five contained a long 'Hallstattian' sword, a prestige item, variously associated with pieces of harness and, in one grave, a bronze bowl with a beaded rim that is curiously similar to ones produced in the 8th century BC by the Villanovan culture of northern Italy.

In 1987 the discovery of a remarkable grave under the Géraud barrow at St-Romain-de-Jalionas (Isère) provided crucial information about conditions in the 9th and 8th centuries BC: traditional objects still in

Found in a warrior's grave at Hallstatt of 400 BC, this decorated sword scabbard (detail above) illustrates the high status of horsemen. A central frieze shows three foot-soldiers with shields followed by four mounted warriors carrying lances and wearing breastplates or jerkins and a skirt over trousers of some sort. Their shoes have upturned toes and they

use were being adapted to new rites, already very close to 6th-century practice. The warrior was buried without a wagon, but with his long bronze sword, gold ornaments and a drinking-set also in bronze: all objects that had previously tended to be reserved for offerings, or which had usually been found grouped together – whether for purposes of ritual or concealment – in late Bronze-Age hoards.

wear protective helmets. To either side two wrestlers hold a wheel, the traditional symbol of prosperity. The tip of the scabbard depicts an erotic scene involving humans and animals.

Long swords

Superseding earlier bronze models, weapons with iron blades were to be the distinctive mark of horsemen or eminent warriors in the 7th century BC. Many such weapons found at Hallstatt confirm they were signs of privilege, with hilts covered in gold leaf or carved in ivory and inlaid with amber.

Towards the end of the 8th and beginning of the 7th century BC, bronze vessels were often placed in graves alongside swords, as in burials at Magny-Lambert and Poiseul-la-Ville (Côte-d'Or). By the end of the 7th century, wagons were put in tombs that also had bronze vessels (La Côte-St-André, Isère).

Jura and Burgundy together mark the south-western limit of the emergent world of the Early Iron Age, although a few outlying settlements have been identified further west in France, in graves around Bourges (Cher) and one at Sublaines (Indre-et-Loire). To the east, especially in the salt-mining area around Hallstatt, there were other cultural centres that had embarked upon a period of economic and social expansion whose influence was decisive.

Lords of white gold

In the Hallstatt cemetery, which has lent its name to the Early Iron Age (mid-8th to end of the 6th century BC), most of the 2000 graves excavated can be dated to the 7th and 6th centuries

A cylindrical bucket (left) nearly 35 cm tall from Magny-Lambert (Côte-d'Or), known as a cordon cist from the circular ribs hammered out around it. This type of bronze vessel was found both north of the Alps and in Italy from the 8th century BC onwards.

Weapons (right) from graves at Hallstatt. The 7th-century BC swords with a long iron blade imitate blades of bronze. Their hilt of organic material was often embellished with ivory, amber or gold.

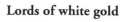

Fibulae with double spirals (above) pinned the clothes of rich women at Hallstatt.

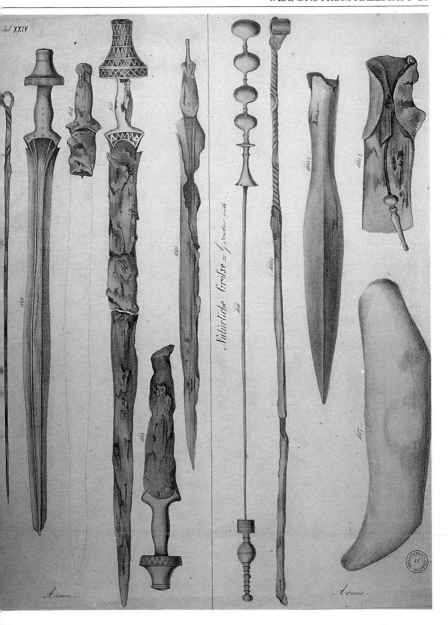

Tab. XXIV

Natürliche Grösse = ⅓ natür voll

Armes.

Armes.

BC. Burials were slightly commoner than cremations, but the latter provided the richest source of goods.

Warriors' graves only made up about a quarter of the cemetery, and of these, only nineteen, from the 8th and 7th centuries BC, produced long swords and ceremonial axes. The more numerous 6th-century graves contained antenna daggers. Women's graves tended to have masses of clanking jewelry and bulky fibulae, typical of the exuberant tastes of the period. Rich graves in the cemetery very often contained impressive sets of bronze vessels, made up of buckets, situlae (buckets with inturned rims), bowls and cups.

Hallstatt could be seen as a well-organized melting-pot whose workforce came from many different areas. There were the miners themselves and the people in charge of them. There were woodcutters and carpenters who collaborated in building the mine, and also rich families of merchants, petty tradesmen and people responsible for the defence of the community. All of these together constructed a new model of an outward-looking society that was in active contact with several different cultures.

Salt, an excellent preservative

Salt was a new form of wealth, an essential feature of sedentary life and object of long-distance trade. It enabled food to be preserved, and was fed to livestock to strengthen them. The northern crest of the Alps has rich reserves of salt. In place-names, the element *Hall,* a synonym of Celtic origin for the German *Salz* (salt), pinpoints the location of very ancient sites of salt exploitation in this region, such as Hallstatt, Hallein, Hall and Reichenhall.

At first the Hallstattians extracted salt from the brine of natural springs by evaporation, but they then went on between the 8th and 6th centuries BC to develop the first and largest centre for mining rock salt from the ground. As early as AD 1311 this place

Various pieces of clothing once worn by miners at Hallein (province of Salzburg) have been found in an exceptional state of preservation due to the surrounding salt. This applies to the shoe shown below and to leather bonnets, also made of carefully stitched calfskin with the fur turned inside.

was being called Heidengebirge ('pagan mountain'), referring to relics of very ancient times that were already being recognized for what they were. Salt is an admirable preservative of organic remains. Items of clothing and protohistoric miners' equipment have survived intact, notably leather rucksacks for transporting blocks of salt, found in 1889, 1939 and 1985. Around 600 BC another big salt mine opened not far from Hallstatt, at Hallein, which had easier access. Hallstatt then went into decline: from the 5th century on it had fewer and less well furnished graves. The scene was now set for developments that were to take place in an area between eastern France and Austria; the prime concern was to reach markets south of the Alps.

Smitten by the Hallstatt cemetery, the Grand Duchess of Mecklenburg got the Emperor Franz Josef's permission to excavate there. She appears below tackling a grave in 1907, surrounded by helpers working more like navvies than archaeologists.

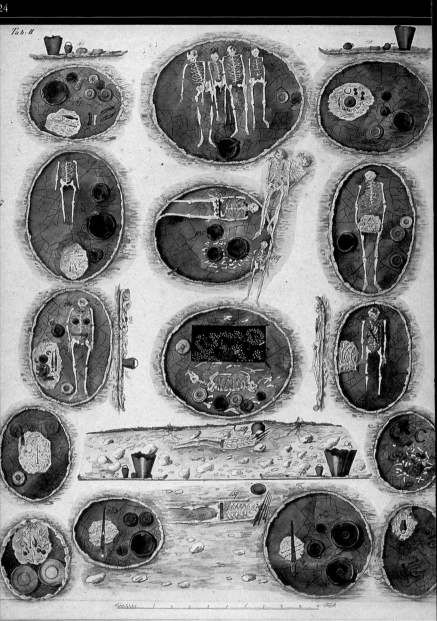

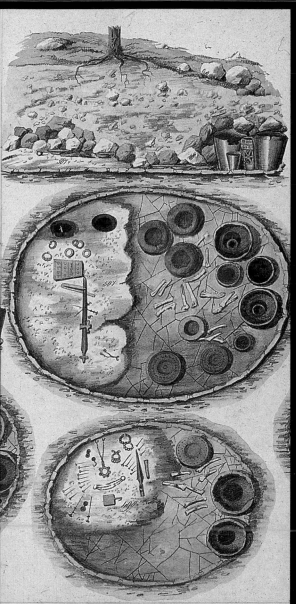

An inveterate excavator

Johann Georg Ramsauer, a mine surveyor, had a veritable field day when he began excavations at the Hallstatt cemetery in 1846. During the next seventeen years he explored 980 graves and unearthed 19,497 objects. He recorded all his observations in letters or notebooks, with watercolour illustrations by his friend Isidor Engel. The Emperor Franz Josef and Empress Elisabeth attended the opening of grave 0⁄ (left) in person in October 1856. Ramsauer, who had no formal training as an archaeologist, was advised by the museum at Linz and then by the Antiquities Collection in Vienna. With his twenty-four children, he was sometimes in financial difficulty at the end of the month, especially when he had had to advance digging expenses. Although he kept most of the material, he, his wife or his companions must sometimes have sold things to wealthy visitors passing through. This would ex   hy objects from Hallstatt can now be found all over the world.

A _Lac de Hallstatt_ — B _Ville de Hallstatt_ — C _Rudolfsturm dominant Hallstatt_ — D _Terrain occup_

The salt mines

The underground galleries of the mine at Hallstatt, some of which existed at the end of the Bronze Age (*c.* 10th–9th centuries BC), were dug into the side of the mountain to follow the veins of salt, and had numerous side passages. They extend for 3750 m over an area of 30,000 m², and the largest reached a depth of 215 m. Similar construction techniques had already been used in the Bronze Age at the Mitterberg copper mines (Austria). Remains of many utensils have been preserved by the salt in these galleries: picks for cutting into the rock, rucksacks for carrying blocks of salt to the surface, wooden tubs for transporting food or water and what may be torches or matches – long resinous sticks that miners are thought to have held between their teeth to shed light while they worked in the galleries.

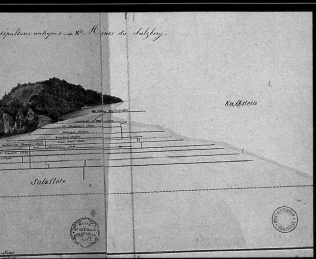

In the 6th century BC, from Burgundy to Austria, the early Celts formed rich settlements run by unified dynasties. An original culture was forged, one that was open to the Mediterranean world. A taste for mead and then wine from Greece or Etruria inspired goldsmiths and craftsmen, who celebrated heroes raised to god-like status.

CHAPTER 2

THE FIRST CELTIC PRINCES

Whether as dancing wrestler on the Hochdorf prince's bronze couch (left) or as life-size ithyphallic sandstone statue (right) that topped the Hirschlanden barrow (Baden-Württemberg), the theme of the warrior-hero crops up in Celtic graves everywhere. The conical hat, gold collar, belt and dagger are characteristic, and are found both in symbolic representations and in grave furnishings.

Around 600 BC the Phocaeans, Greeks who had originally settled in Asia Minor in the 10th century BC, founded Massalia (now Marseilles) in southern France. This was to be a focal point for further coastal colonization. At the same time the first Celtic cultural centre was developing deep within a broad expanse of western central Europe. Throughout the 6th century BC it was conspicuous by its wealth, its brilliant clan-based society ruled by powerful princes and the dynamism of its culture. These new groups were organized in very much the same way from Burgundy to Austria. Their most important figures were princes who were buried wearing gold collars in wagon graves, each under a huge funerary mound.

They were already known to the Greeks. Hecataeus of Miletus, an Ionian geographer and writer from Asia Minor, mentioned the Celts by name for the first time in the 6th century BC as being neighbours of the Ligurians, implying that they were settled to the north of Provence. In the next century Herodotus

placed the Celts around the Danube and beyond the Pillars of Hercules (Gibraltar).

Rich citadels north of the Alps

The birth of this new society was marked by the establishment of citadels on high places that overlooked vast tracts of land. Among the most important of these places, a dozen were probably residences of princes or territorial chiefs who played a key role not only in the economy and politics of

The Hohenasperg (left) in all its glory, dominating a vast landscape. At its foot, various Celtic princes were buried under thirteen barrows within a radius of 25 km. It may have been the seat of the Hochdorf prince.

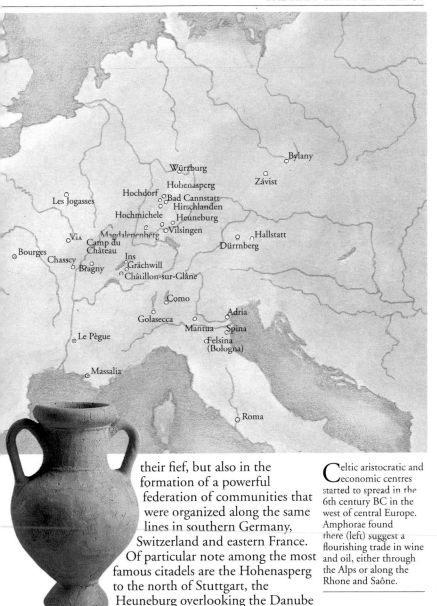

Bylany

Würzburg

Závist

Hohenasperg

Hochdorf Bad Cannstatt
           Hirschlanden

Les Jogasses

Hochmichele Heuneburg

Via   Magdalenenberg Vilsingen   Hallstatt

Camp du
Château   Dürrnberg

Bourges   Ins

Chassy   Grächwill

Bragny   Châtillon-sur-Glâne

Como

Adria

Golasecca   Spina

Le Pègue   Mantua   Felsina
                      (Bologna)

Massalia

Roma

their fief, but also in the formation of a powerful federation of communities that were organized along the same lines in southern Germany, Switzerland and eastern France. Of particular note among the most famous citadels are the Hohenasperg to the north of Stuttgart, the Heuneburg overlooking the Danube

Celtic aristocratic and economic centres started to spread in the 6th century BC in the west of central Europe. Amphorae found there (left) suggest a flourishing trade in wine and oil, either through the Alps or along the Rhone and Saône.

near Sigmaringen, Uetliberg near Zurich, Châtillon-sur-Glâne near Fribourg and Mont Lassois (Côte-d'Or), to name but a few.

On level ground, other sites more recently discovered have yielded material exactly like that from the citadels, in particular Mediterranean imports. These places may be trading posts, as at Bragny-sur-Loire (Saône-et-Loire), or other forms of princely settlement, as at Bourges (Cher), where several graves with imported bronze vessels were found during the 19th century.

Some aspects of this Early Iron-Age civilization are spectacular: there was a new profusion of exotic products imported from the south, complex and solemn rites were conducted at funeral ceremonies and there was a strong personal bias in dynastic power. Yet little is known about the palaces of these princes, since none of the citadels excavated so far has yielded one. There are, however, a few hints. At the Wittnauerhorn in Switzerland two central buildings, larger than the others, might have been the residence of rulers, while at the base of one of the barrows at Giessübel-Talhau, not far from the Heuneburg, the plan of a vast dwelling may have been identified.

The Heuneburg

The Heuneburg is the most extensively excavated of these citadels. Its rampart presents some startling features. A wall 4 m high, made of sun-dried mud-bricks on a stone base, was furnished with projecting bastions, architecture wholly exceptional north of the Alps, but well known in the Mediterranean world (for instance at Gela in Sicily). Might this be the work of an expatriate Greek

The hydria was a vessel intended for the water that was mixed with concentrated wine. One from Grächwill (below), near Bern (Switzerland), was probably made at a Spartan colony in c. 570 BC and presumably held drink for the funeral rites. At its neck, a figure of the winged mistress of animals recalls ancient oriental symbols of fertility and immortality and the Greek Artemis.

architect or of a Celt who had learnt his trade south of the Alps? Inside the village, houses were distributed along narrow streets. Outside, an agglomeration surrounded this acropolis. Many sherds of black- and red-figure pottery mingled with Greek amphorae or Etruscan products. It seems there were brilliant local craftsmen. Not only did the Heuneburg potters have proper fast-spinning potters' wheels, but the metalsmiths were able to reproduce or repair imported products, as shown by the clay mould for an Etruscan oenochoe (wine flagon) handle join found on the site. Does this represent assimilation of techniques or the introduction of foreign workmen?

Built on a promontory above the Danube Valley, the Heuneburg fortress (above) was surrounded by 11 tumuli within a 5-km radius. With its square towers and 600 m of mud-brick wall built in the 6th century BC on a stone base – a Mediterranean technique – it raises questions about the movement of craftsmen. So does the curious mould for a wine-flagon handle join (left) also found there: locally made, it has a satyr's head, a motif that the Etruscans liked on their flagons.

Funerals fit for kings

The largest barrow of this period is the Magdalenenberg, near the Kapf settlement in the Black Forest, an area rich in iron ore. It is over 100 m in diameter and soon attracted covetous attention, like the Hohmichele, the oldest barrow, ascribed to the founder of the Heuneburg. These graves were robbed only a few years after the funerals. At the Magdalenenberg, dendrochronological analysis of the walls of the funerary chamber dates the burial to 550 BC. The tomb was gutted in 504 BC, as evidenced by wooden pieces of tools abandoned on the spot by their ghoulish owners.

Usually the primary tomb, in the centre, belongs to the prince. This was a vast log-built funerary chamber surrounded by secondary tombs – probably for relatives or family members – that went on being used for one or two generations.

The presence of a funerary wagon is the most original feature of these princely graves. These were four-wheeled ceremonial carts designed to move slowly. Were they only used for funerals or also for processions during a prince's lifetime? Curiously, the wheels of some wagons were taken off and arranged along the wall of the funerary chamber.

The dead man's sacrificed wife might share his grave, as at Hohmichele (Germany). The drawing below is a reconstruction based on the arrangement of the tomb when it was opened. The woman lay under the wagon's wheels and the man beside them; the body of the wagon may have been taken apart for him to lie on.

Designed to move slowly and above all straight ahead, the funerary wagons of Celtic princes had a fixed steering shaft. Analysis of wood from several wagons shows that species were carefully selected for different parts.

For a long time the models for these Hallstattian wagons were thought to have come from Italy. Yet, despite similarities in funerary rites, the Celtic wagons are made differently. To the north of the Alps ritual carts or symbolic wheels had already been used for religious purposes for several generations. The ritual wagon seems to descend from ancient local Bronze-Age beliefs. Sometimes accompanied by a wife who had been ritually killed, the dead man was adorned with his personal ornaments and symbols of power.

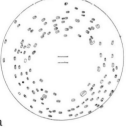

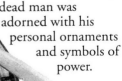

The Kaltbrunn barrow (top) was excavated on the orders of Grand Duke Frederick of Baden in 1864. Below it is a typical plan of an Iron-Age grave mound, a sort of family or tribal vault. The prince's grave is in the centre, and secondary burials were placed around it until another family or tribe rose to power and a different barrow was used.

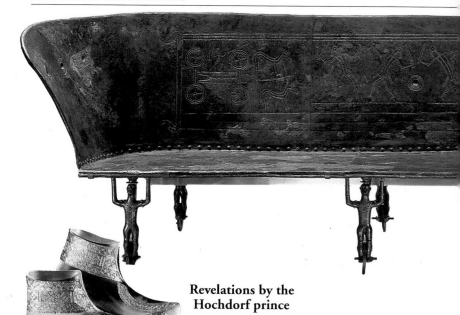

Revelations by the Hochdorf prince

Painstaking excavation of a princely tomb in the village of Hochdorf, a few kilometres from Stuttgart, has yielded priceless information. The inside walls of the funerary chamber, built of oak logs, each measured 4.7 m. Cloths were spread on the ground and draped on the walls, fixed in place with iron hooks and pinned together with fibulae.

The prince, around forty years of age, was tall for his period (1.87 m), and was buried between 540 and 520 BC with especially rich offerings because of his importance. He was lying, unusually, not on his wagon but on a couch of sheet bronze that stands on little wheels. His clothing was secured by bronze and gold fibulae, he was wearing a hat of

It has been noticed that many princely graves contained people who were above the average height of their contemporaries. The Hochdorf prince was tall in this way; his skull (below) was large and his facial features broad and generous. Although the cause of his death at a rather advanced age for his time is not known, it does seem likely that he suffered from arthritis. The prince's leather boots (above left) were covered in embossed gold leaf during the funeral ceremony; they came up to his ankles and probably turned up at the toes.

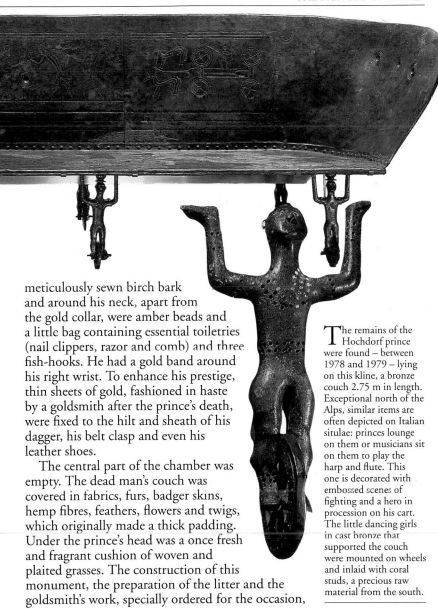

meticulously sewn birch bark and around his neck, apart from the gold collar, were amber beads and a little bag containing essential toiletries (nail clippers, razor and comb) and three fish-hooks. He had a gold band around his right wrist. To enhance his prestige, thin sheets of gold, fashioned in haste by a goldsmith after the prince's death, were fixed to the hilt and sheath of his dagger, his belt clasp and even his leather shoes.

The central part of the chamber was empty. The dead man's couch was covered in fabrics, furs, badger skins, hemp fibres, feathers, flowers and twigs, which originally made a thick padding. Under the prince's head was a once fresh and fragrant cushion of woven and plaited grasses. The construction of this monument, the preparation of the litter and the goldsmith's work, specially ordered for the occasion,

The remains of the Hochdorf prince were found – between 1978 and 1979 – lying on this kline, a bronze couch 2.75 m in length. Exceptional north of the Alps, similar items are often depicted on Italian situlae: princes lounge on them or musicians sit on them to play the harp and flute. This one is decorated with embossed scenes of fighting and a hero in procession on his cart. The little dancing girls in cast bronze that supported the couch were mounted on wheels and inlaid with coral studs, a precious raw material from the south.

give some idea of the length of time it took to prepare for such funeral ceremonies.

Drinking-horns and mead

The large set of drinking equipment in the tomb included nine drinking-horns hung along one wall. They, too, were specially decorated for the occasion with strips of gold foil. The largest, an iron horn 1.20 m long and holding 5.5 litres, was undoubtedly the dead man's own possession. At his feet a bronze cauldron that holds 500 litres and is decorated with lion figurines stood on a wooden tripod. A golden cup used for dipping into it was balanced on its rim. The brownish remains in the bottom of the great cauldron have revealed it was used for a brew of mead at the farewell feast. Pollen analysis suggests a beverage based on honey and spiced with local plants such as thyme, mountain jasmine, plantain, knapweed and meadowsweet.

On the wagon trimmed with iron mounts, the banqueting service was completed with bronze bowls and plates. An axe, two knives and an iron spearhead were also placed there, as were pieces of harness and a long wooden goad.

The symposium ceremony

The Hochdorf cauldron, whose lions certainly came from Greek workshops, is one of the objects that demonstrate the existence of long-distance trade in ornamental goods with Mediterranean countries. The hydria (water jar, see p. 32) from Grächwill (Switzerland) and the krater (large vase in which concentrated wine was diluted, see p. 42) from Vix (Côte-d'Or) are among the most famous imported drinking utensils

Sets of vessels for food and drink were usually put into the funerary chamber. Drinking-horns, large bronze or pottery dishes, cauldrons and buckets of native design were gradually replaced by wine-drinking wares imported from Greece, Etruria or southern Italy, such as wine flagons or basins decorated with griffin heads and standing on tripods (below). At Hochdorf the prince's drinking-horn (left) stood out from among others made of the usual animal material as much by its size as by the fact that it is made of wrought iron.

used for symposium ceremonies. A very ancient ritual in the Hallstattian world, and also practised by the Greeks, this was a banquet at which the dead man's faithful companions assembled for one last time. Plenty of bronze vessels of local manufacture have also been found in cemeteries, especially at Hallstatt.

A taste for wine

New contacts with the south introduced wine, a drink previously unknown north of the Alps, and one that

As the Hochdorf tomb (reconstruction above) remained intact until 1978, many observations could be made on the spot. Painstaking excavation and laboratory analyses have even determined that mead was contained in the cauldron below.

was to have important cultural repercussions. The Celts loved it. Wine soon became one of the mainsprings of trade with the Mediterranean world. It was transported as a spiced concentrate in amphorae, plentiful remains of which are found on settlement sites. From 500 BC onwards wine would replace traditional mead at symposia: there were traces of wine in the bottom of the prince of Hallein's bronze flask.

Greek and Etruscan vessels, including the famous wine flagons, were refinements that went with wine drinking – or drunkenness – at princes' festival and funeral meals.

Gold and power

A golden collar or torque was the supreme symbol of princely power. Made of sheets of beaten gold, collars were usually decorated with small stamped geometric motifs, a legacy of Bronze-Age abstract art. They are found on the neck of the Hirschlanden statue (Baden-Württemberg, see p. 29) and on chiefs buried in the richest wagon graves; the latter, armed with a dagger, commonly sport a gold bracelet on the right

Exceptional in shape and size (51 cm high), the prince of Hallein's flask (left) was mounted on human-like legs and still contained traces of wine. The Etruscan wine flagon below is from Lake Como.

arm. These privileged men also often had a gold cup, resting on the rim of the vessel that contained the drink. Apart from these prestige goods, used while the princes were alive, some objects placed in their graves were covered in gold during the funeral rites. The goldsmith must have worked close to the barrow, using, as at Hochdorf, a set of small stamps whose identical impressions can be found on various different items.

Even in the richest women's graves, those of wives of princes or members of their family, gold is not as evident. It is only used to decorate their hair in the form of large spherical pin heads or loops that held a veil around their faces.

Gold was imbued with the Celts' sense of identity. Native gold products always held a deep meaning, so the Celts had no need to import other jewelry. The influence of Mediterranean goldsmiths' work can only be traced in the sporadic adoption of techniques like soldering, granulation and filigree, used to perfection by Celtic goldsmiths. The Vix collar (p. 43) is a good example.

The bead and pendant (below) found near Bern are oddly like Etruscan products.

The princes' gold torque (below) recalls the abstract art of the Bronze Age. High-ranking women had bracelets, beads, large-headed pins or earrings of hammered and embossed gold leaf.

The extravagant princess of Vix

At the foot of Mont Lassois (Côte-d'Or), the most extraordinary Celtic tomb discovered in France in the 20th century belonged to a woman about thirty-five years of age who died around 480 BC. This woman was undoubtedly as powerful as the greatest princes of her time. She was lying in the body of a small wagon whose wheels had been removed. Beside it was an enormous bronze krater, probably from Magna Graecia, with a large lid. Several other vessels had been placed on its rim: a silver phiale (cup) with a gilded boss, protected in a fibre covering, two Attic cups and a bronze Etruscan wine flagon. Along one

The Vix princess seems to have died aged about 35. Her features could be reconstructed from her skull and jawbone.

The largest known krater of antiquity, from Vix, is 1.64 m high, 208 kg in weight and holds 1100 litres. Concentrated wine was mixed with water in it: at the top, a strainer filtered out the herbs and spices that flavoured the wine. On its rim stood, among other things, an Attic cup (below) for sampling the result.

wall were some Etruscan bowls that bear
a striking resemblance
to ones depicted in
frescoes at Tarquinia.
On the ground blue
and red pigments came
from cloths or
decorative
paintings.

The princess was adorned in
local style – she wore a
collar of large stone and
amber beads, bronze ankle
rings, lignite bracelets and fibulae with coral
studs. At her neck was a strange and unique
ornament of pure gold, taken at first for a diadem.
In fact it turned out to be a massive torque, a
masterpiece by a Celtic goldsmith familiar with
Mediterranean techniques. This attraction for
things from the south is typical of the period
of the earliest Celtic
princes, when craftsmen
would go to the extent
of imitating articles such as wine flagons.

Trade among equals

Skilled crafts developed in the Alpine salt- and
copper-mining areas. Iron ore, which is much more
widely distributed geographically, was exploited fairly
early on, especially in areas like Lorraine and
Burgundy that played a major role in shaping the
culture of the Early Iron Age. There is no surviving

Recent X-rays of the
Vix princess' torque
(480 g of pure gold)
have revealed that it was
made from about twenty
pieces carefully
assembled by a master-
craftsman familiar with
Mediterranean
techniques but faithful
to Celtic traditions. Its
little winged horses (a
theme also found on the
Hochdorf collar and on
stamped sheet bronze at
Hallstatt) were made by
the lost-wax process.
The filigree and beaded
threads they stand on are
only 0.2 mm thick.
Oddly in such a jewel,
the round terminals are
attached to the collar by
rings bearing stamped
decoration of local
workmanship.

material evidence for the techniques of iron extraction or forging used at that time, but it is clear that blacksmiths were already able to make wheel hoops and wagon trappings. Bronze-working was now restricted to personal ornaments and tableware. Potters worked at family or village level. For the most part their products were hand-shaped and were colourfully decorated with red haematite, white chalk or glossy black graphite. Imported raw materials such as amber, lignite, coral and ivory were worked by specialized craftsmen attached to princely courts.

The early Celtic centres with their marked hierarchical organization were essentially nodal points on long-range trading networks that led through the Alpine passes or along the Rhone Valley. Their choice of imports was selective: the Celts would not let Greek and Etruscan merchants dictate to them, but decided for themselves which goods they needed to satisfy their taste in luxuries or which goods fitted in with traditional regional rituals that had been handed down from Bronze-Age times. The colonial model that used to be invoked has now been abandoned: the Greeks and Etruscans dealt with the Celts as equals.

Metalworkers ranked highest of all craftsmen: first came the blacksmiths, then bronzesmiths, coppersmiths and metal casters. There is little evidence for techniques of iron extraction or for the workshops themselves, but smiths were certainly able to make wheel hoops and cart trappings. Bronzesmiths specialized in making personal ornaments and utensils. Potters, whose workshops were probably sited close to their sources of clay, produced at family or village level. Pots were hand-fashioned and had coloured decoration in red haematite, white chalk or glossy black graphite.

At La Ronce (Loiret) this bronze bucket covered in several layers of cloth served as a receptacle for the ashes of a cremation burial under a barrow. A rite that involved covering the grave goods in fabric has often been observed and probably indicates an ultimate concern to preserve the dead person's possessions.

Specialized craftsmen attached to the prince's court worked imported raw materials – amber, lignite, coral and ivory – while the glass industry was in full swing.

Glass beads from Slovenia (left), an area adjoining the eastern Celtic zone. Where the Halstattian world was in contact with the Adriatic area, women were very fond of eye motifs and of the colours of these rare products that brightened up their finery.

The latter, after all, had ample to export in return: salt, tin, copper, amber, wool, hides, furs and gold.

Traditional style in Illyrian vein

The Early Iron-Age Celts can be divided into two geographical groups: the western Hallstattian zone

Amber from the Baltic was the raw material for many Celtic necklaces (left). Probably exchanged for salt, it was the object of regular trade with the north.

The wide belts of sheet bronze worn by the first Celts were stamped with repetitive geometric motifs (left) like those later used on princes' collars.

where swords were worn, and an eastern Hallstattian zone where axes were carried. The same division applies in the artistic sphere, especially in the decoration of objects like pottery whose overall shape is otherwise similar. In the western zone abstract art of Bronze-Age ancestry prevails, while a more narrative style tended to emerge in the eastern zone.

Already in the 7th century BC urns from Sopron (Hungary) and Fischbach (Bavaria) were displaying schematic silhouettes of dancers, musicians, weavers, women with raised arms and warriors. On vessels of hammered bronze from the cemetery of Kleinklein (eastern Austria) this figurative trend mixes in with the geometric tradition, and there are processions of people and mythical hunts.

One of the graves in the cemetery even included a human mask and severed hands made of sheet bronze that were influenced by the Illyrian

The stag and wild boar were favourite Celtic beasts. With other figurines of animals or warrior-heroes, this tiny bronze boar (left), measuring 5.6 cm, was found in a votive deposit at the sanctuary of Balzers (Liechtenstein).

This 7th-century BC Bavarian pot from Fischbach has shadowy figures of people or animals pricked into the clay, still in a rigid geometric style.

The small (48 cm) cult wagon from Strettweg, Austria, brings together many Celtic sacred images. A nature goddess, bearing a scent burner, is surrounded by mounted warriors and men holding stags by their antlers.

world nearby – funerary masks of the same period but made in gold foil have been found at Trebeniste in Macedonia (former Yugoslavia).

Similar figures with obvious mythological significance – including a large goddess and ithyphallic warriors together with animals (in this case stags, but sometimes wild boars) – form a scene on the cult wagon placed in a cremation grave at Strettweg (Austria).

Situla art

A taste for representing narrative scenes on vessels or belt clasps goes back to the 7th century BC and started in Etruria. Designs enlivened by griffins, sphinxes, lions and grazing stags and various plant motifs spread towards the Adriatic where they developed into a form called situla art. One of the earliest of these decorated bronze buckets, dated *c.*

Master bronzesmiths north of the Alps carried on the art of situla decoration and illustrated familiar heroic entertainments: sporting contests or, as on the situla – decorated bronze bucket – from Kuffarn (Austria), the satisfaction of a prince in a wide-brimmed hat who holds out his cup to a servant pouring wine, while behind him a companion goes to refill two empty containers (left).

Situlae were buckets made of hammered sheet bronze with incurved rims and sometimes a lid. Situla art was confined to the Adriatic, Etruria and Slovenia before it spread to the eastern Alps.

650 BC, comes from Este (northern Italy). The workshops that specialized in making these situlae were confined to northern Slovenia. With their stunning mastery of repoussé work and chasing, the bronzesmiths portrayed scenes from the heavenly afterlife that lay in store for warrior-heroes: feasts, processions, hunts, spectacles of games and fights, and other pleasures, with women taking the role of servants pouring drinks. Situla art played an important part in the genesis of Celtic art. The theme of the deified hero, dear to the Celts, put in its next appearance on the fringe of the western zone, at Hirschlanden and Hochdorf in southern Germany.

In 6th- and 5th-century BC Slovenia, decorated bronze plaques ornamented the wide belts of men of high rank. One from Magdalenska Gora (Slovenia) shows a horseman and boxers with dumb-bells (above left). These face one another on either side of a plumed helmet that seems to belong to the symbolic world of Iron-Age warriors; examples are also sometimes found in votive deposits in the Alps. A detail from the belt plaque from Vače (Slovenia) shows a foot-soldier wearing the same helmet and bearing a shield, axe and two lances (left).

Famous for their courage, fearless warriors seized Rome and then launched an assault on Delphi. But these mad conquests lasted less than a century. The Celts never achieved truly centralized power or an empire in the political sense of the word, yet they left a lasting mark upon the different peoples they encountered.

CHAPTER 3
THE ALL-CONQUERING CELTS

Very gradually the water-bird motifs of the Bronze Age gave way to doves and then birds of prey (fibula from Hallein, right). At the same time images of the Celts reflect increasing aggression and lust for wealth (left, detail from the Civitalba frieze).

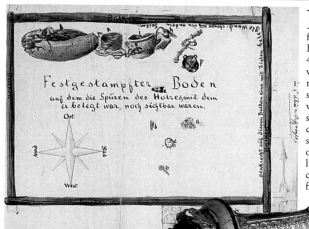

Near the Hohenasperg a final burial was made at Kleinaspergle in about 450 BC (recorded in watercolour, left). It recalled its predecessors' splendour (imported wares: an Etruscan stamnos and two Attic cups), but also displayed symbols of the new type of power (locally made luxury goods: a native copy of a bronze wine flagon, two gold-plated drinking-horns,

a ribbed bronze bucket, a large bronze cauldron and a baldric fitting decorated in gold and coral).

The power of the Early Iron-Age princes crumbled after two or three generations. Whether because of an internal crisis, a reorganization of trading networks or conflict between Greeks and Etruscans for control of trade, the citadels that had fostered commercial relations were abandoned around 500 BC in favour of a more rural way of life, now governed by warrior chieftains.

A few of the old centres, like the Hohenasperg, held out for a little longer, but all eventually collapsed. On their margins, during the 5th century, new regions came to the fore as focal points of civilization: the Rhineland with the Hunsrück–Eifel culture, Bohemia, Champagne and the Ardennes.

Social levelling

Customs and material culture slowly changed. Etruscan stamnoi (vases for pure wine) are found in rich 5th-century graves: at La Motte-St-Valentin (Haute-Marne) or Altrier (Luxembourg). Mirrors imported from Etruria or their imitations were luxuries often placed in women's graves, as at

The ram, symbolic of strength, was often used as an ornamental theme in Celtic art. Its head formed the tip of the mid-5th-century Kleinaspergle drinking-horn, whose mount (above) is 17 cm long and made of iron, bronze and gold.

Uetliberg, near Zurich or again at La Motte-St-Valentin. These grave furnishings suggest that the social distance had lessened between those in positions of relative power and the rest of the people. Mediterranean imports dropped off and the jewelry worn was less sumptuous. Chiefs' burials had lost their monumental character and lavish show of wealth, though they still retained a standard range of goods.

The Late Iron Age seems to have been a more democratic period, but also more warlike. The ceremonial dagger, symbol of power of the early Celts, gave way to the complete armoury of the warrior. Princes, or rather warrior-aristocrats like the lord of Hallein, were buried on a two-wheeled chariot – a fighting vehicle designed for speed – and no longer on a ceremonial wagon.

Following Etruscan custom, mirrors became essential accessories for women of the 5th-century Celtic aristocracy, who took them to the grave (above, mirror from La Motte-St-Valentin, Haute-Marne).

The cradles of Celtic art

From the end of the 6th until the middle of the 4th century BC a small group of Celts in the Hunsrück and Eifel hills on the left bank of the Rhine stood out particularly in terms of both their dynamism and their conservatism.

They had the greatest concentration of rich graves in that period, placed under barrows, often in groups,

With two oars and upturned prow, this miniature gold boat (6.6 cm long) came from a warrior's grave on the Dürrnberg (Austria). It has the traditional shape of vessels that in the Iron Age carried salt, among other things, and still today ply the lakes of the Salzkammergut.

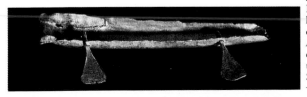

and sometimes related to defended settlements. Several princes were buried there by rites typical of the early Celts north-west of the Alps, with torques, bracelets, fibulae and belt and chariot fittings in bronze or iron, and gold mounts on drinking vessels, all decorated in the early Celtic style. A bronze or especially a gold bracelet, sometimes lavishly decorated, was for a long time to remain a mark of nobility for one category of high-ranking warriors. A small number, including that of the prince of Kleinaspergle (Württemberg), had an iron or gold-plated bronze trimming with coral studs.

Further east, in Bohemia, the same civilization blossomed. Defended villages were built or rebuilt, as at Závist. The Celtic princes of Bohemia sported the same personal ornaments as

The Schwarzenbach tomb contained a small sheet-gold face (below) and a fine openwork gold mount (bottom left) that probably once encased a wooden bowl.

Two female faces (above right) make terminals for a gold torque from Reinheim (Sarre). They are topped by objects resembling big ears or mistletoe leaves (as is the face above) between which is the head of a bird of prey, and by two pear-shaped buds. This jewel made from many pieces soldered together must have been worn by its powerful owner in the mid-4th century.

their Rhineland cousins, as shown by an individual buried at Chlum, though the Celts of Champagne did not follow this practice.

Exceptional women

Between the Sarre and the Rhineland-Palatinate it is common for rich barrow graves to contain drinking wares embellished with precious metal: mounts and lids for drinking-horns, or wooden cups like that from Schwarzenbach (Sarre) covered in gold tracery.

Princely burials of women attain fresh prominence, with spectacular furnishings: one at Bad Dürkheim with an Etruscan tripod and stamnos and a golden torque and bracelet, and of course the treasures of the princesses of Reinheim and Waldalgesheim, one of whom lived at the beginning and the other at the end of the 4th century BC.

A s in Etruria, precious vessels were placed on bronze tripods, often with lion's feet. The tripod and bronze stamnos (below) from the princely tomb at Bad Dürkheim (Rhineland) were Etruscan imports in the 5th century BC.

All these women who have been discovered surrounded by the tell-tale marks of rank must, like the princess of Vix, have played a part equal to that of the greatest Celtic chiefs.

The nonconformism of Champagne

The vast Late Iron-Age cemeteries of Champagne are made up of flat graves without barrows (sign of a dense population) that are deeply dug into the chalky soil. Easy to find, these sites were already being excavated

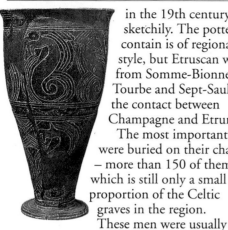

in the 19th century, often very sketchily. The pottery they contain is of regional 'Marnian' style, but Etruscan wine flagons from Somme-Bionne, Somme-Tourbe and Sept-Saulx show the contact between Champagne and Etruria.

The most important men were buried on their chariots – more than 150 of them, which is still only a small proportion of the Celtic graves in the region.

These men were usually armed and wore a bronze helmet. The decorative parts of their horses' harness were placed in their grave. The more numerous infantry warriors only had their arms: a sword, spears and javelins. Women had belt clasps, fibulae that pinned their clothes, and other symbolic jewelry such as the torque that seems to have had religious meaning.

The 5th and early 4th centuries BC were a time of great stability, which was reflected in material goods. The society was fairly egalitarian, though more women's graves exist due to the progressive departure of men for other horizons.

Emergence of a unique style

In the 5th century BC technical innovations allowed

Typical of work in 5th-century BC Champagne, a large vase from La Cheppe (left) is decorated with monstrous incised eels. Pointed helmets, like the one below from Berru (Marne) of the early 4th century BC, were now among the arms buried with princes on two-wheeled war chariots.

the Celts
to depart
conclusively
from the
repetitive geometric art
that had been very much in vogue in many areas
during the Early Iron Age. Now lines flowed freely,
and the assimilation of Mediterranean influences
reached perfection.

Phalerae were discs, usually of bronze, that decorated horse harnesses or chariots. One from Cuperly (Marne) was 10 cm in diameter and came from the grave of a rich warrior buried in the late 5th or early 4th century BC (left). It is made up of a number of different pieces, notably openwork bosses in relief; the perfect arrangement of the design is due to its preparation with compasses. Simpler, but also larger, are the phalerae from St-Jean-sur-Tourbe (Marne), 24.5 cm in diameter (below).

Oriental themes were introduced: the tree of life surrounded by birds, monstrous guardians or dragons, the lord of the beasts, palmettes, lotus flowers and human masks. Found from Champagne to Bohemia and within the Carpathians, these motifs hint at profound changes in belief and form new magical symbols that remained a part of Celtic artists' repertoire.

The introduction of dry-point compasses allowed complex new patterns to be made. A marked taste for ambiguity, multiple readings and the interplay of lines and shapes at the expense of natural forms, something that doubtless echoed other trends in Celtic thought, became fundamental elements in the decorative art that embellished the valuables of the élite.

Regional imagery

These widely shared common themes had different regional interpretations. Fibulae with a symmetrical double mask were mainly produced in the middle Rhineland, while ones with an asymmetrical bow were mostly made in the east. The wild boar, a bird in flight or fibulae shaped like a shoe came from the Dürrnberg workshops (Austria). Fantastic figurative designs are most common in Bohemia but are relatively rare in Switzerland and Champagne, which are both areas with less exuberant tastes.

This first style (in the 5th and early 4th centuries BC) was also adapted to pottery. In Champagne and the Ardennes wheel-turned pedestal vases are painted in bold red curvilinear designs. In Armorica (Brittany) black pottery mimics the shapes of metal vessels and is decorated with stamped motifs or incised designs based on the palmette.

On this pedestal vase (left) from Prunay (Marne) the curving design was made with a slip (a clay coating rich in metallic oxides) which produces contrasting red and black when fired.

The urge to migrate

According to legend, the Celts of Gaul at this time were under the rule of the Bituriges and their king, Ambigatus. Anxious to relieve his kingdom of excess population, he decided to send his nephews Bellovesus and Segovesus, enterprising young men, to make new homes in whatever direction the gods would choose. The oracle allotted the German Hercynian forest to Segovesus and Italy to Bellovesus. In fact at the end of the 5th century BC some Celtic chiefs did embark upon a process of conquest of all the middle latitudes of Europe, followed by Mediterranean Europe as well. The Celts' fascination with Italy and the confused situation into which Italy had fallen as Etruscan power declined marked it out as a prime target for invasion. Starting from north of the Alps, bands of Celts streamed into the peninsula. They did not feel like strangers, since the existing populations of the Italian Alps were often of Celtic stock. The newcomers' tracks can easily be traced: objects such as belt clasps indicate Celtic warriors were present in Languedoc in the 5th century BC, en route for Italy, into which they filtered gradually as scouts or as mercenaries seeking employment.

An anthropomorphic fibula (left) from a Bohemian grave of the second half of the 5th century BC may represent a specific Celtic mythological figure. His bronze body is riddled with holes which probably originally held coral studs.

The faces on the page opposite are two parts of a single late 5th-century BC Slovakian fibula. This type of triple human mask was widespread, especially in central Europe. Two masks face each other, their chins on the bow of the brooch; a third is joined at the forehead to the larger face, where there is also a setting for a missing stud, probably of coral. Perfect examples of classical Celtic art, the eyebrows swirl back from the nose to the top of the brow.

Assimilation of new motifs by the Transalpine Celts and the important role of northern Italy in the transformation of Celtic art can be traced through openwork belt clasps. This one from Bavaria (left) uses the oriental theme of the tree of life.

A host of strange creatures

At the beginning of the Late Iron Age a whole bestiary, including horses, wild boars and birds, was created on small objects. Fibulae and other ornaments were decorated with heads of men, animals or fantastic creatures whose combination sheds light on the Celts' symbolic system. On human faces the mouth and eyebrows are accentuated, while eyes and cheeks protrude. Hair and beards take vegetal form. Ears become pointed. Shown here, starting from the far left, are two 5th-century BC fibulae from Hallein, one with a twin image of an ass's head at one end and a grotesque human head at the other, and one in the form of a bird with hooked beak; then a wine flagon handle join from Kleinaspergle with a half-human, half-bestial face; a sumptuous human-headed horse from the lid of the Reinheim flagon; a detail from the gold bracelet of the Rodenbach warrior; a decorative 4th-century BC harness buckle from the tomb of the Waldalgesheim princess, with two confronted flamingoes; and a 2nd-century BC cast-bronze terret ring with a hallucinating face.

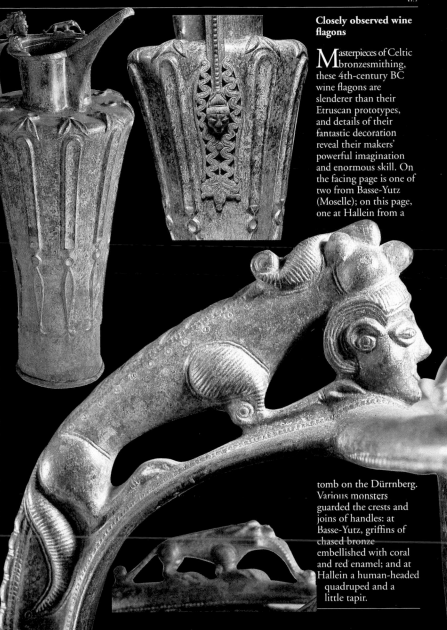

Closely observed wine flagons

Masterpieces of Celtic bronzesmithing, these 4th-century BC wine flagons are slenderer than their Etruscan prototypes, and details of their fantastic decoration reveal their makers' powerful imagination and enormous skill. On the facing page is one of two from Basse-Yutz (Moselle); on this page, one at Hallein from a tomb on the Dürrnberg. Various monsters guarded the crests and joins of handles: at Basse-Yutz, griffins of chased bronze embellished with coral and red enamel; and at Hallein a human-headed quadruped and a little tapir.

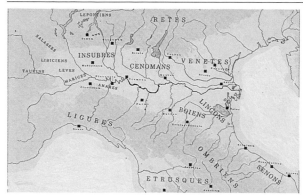

The Celts invade Italy

Conquests really began in earnest at the beginning of the 4th century BC: 300,000 Celts were on the move after this sort of *ver sacrum* (a ritual exodus, described by ancient authors, in which part of the population is marked out for foreign colonization).

Relations with other peoples shifted from the commercial and peaceful to the political and warlike, although the situation was probably very complex. While ancient texts mainly describe wars between the Celts and the Romans or the way Celtic mercenaries profited from Mediterranean cities' internal conflicts, archaeological evidence presents a different picture in which the new arrivals fitted easily into Italian life – Celtic and Italian culture met in a true symbiosis.

Celtic tribes in Italy: Insubres at the foot of the Alps with their capital at Mediolanum (Milan); Cenomani around Verona and in the Po Valley, with their capital at Brixia (Brescia); Boii around Parma and Bologna; and Lingones on the Adriatic coast. The Senones were last to arrive in Italy, and their graves show strong Greco-Roman influence. The helmet (below) from Canosa di Puglia (Bari) proves the Celts were present in southern Italy between 367 and 349 BC.

The Eternal City in barbarian hands

The first wave of Celtic immigrants settled a substantial area of the Po valley in Italy. Expansion southwards began about 400 BC and the Celts laid siege to Clusium (now Chiusi). Another expedition, mainly the work of the Senones, a Celtic people from the Yonne basin in France, marched upon Rome. The year 386 BC was marred by a series of tragic events: a Roman defeat a few kilometres from the city at the confluence of the Allia and Tiber, then the destruction of Rome itself, which was sacked, burnt down and occupied for seven months.

The Celts laid siege to, and would have taken, the Capitol, had the famous geese not sounded the alert. Warriors swept into every part of the city where they thought there might be rich spoils. They spared the Romans no shame, and set a ransom of 1000 pounds of gold. The Gauls used loaded weights, but when a tribune complained, Brennus, the conquering hero, added his sword to the weights on the scales with the cynical words, 'Woe to the defeated'.

The Celts' adventure in Italy made an early and lasting impression upon artists. Above: *The Gauls in Sight of Rome* by Evariste Luminais. Below: a stele from Bormio near Lake Como, an area where inscriptions in a Celtic language and alphabet first appeared in the 4th century BC.

'Finding the poorer houses locked up but the nobles' mansions wide open, they were almost more hesitant to enter the open ones than to break into the others: they felt a sort of awe in seeing, seated in their courtyards, those figures whose costume lent them a superhuman grandeur.... The Gauls stood frozen before them as before statues in a temple, until one of them, a certain Marcus Papirius, whose beard a warrior had touched ... hit him over the head with his ivory staff. This unleashed his assailant's anger, and Papirius was killed with all the others, still in their seats.... The Gauls looted the houses and, after stripping them, set them on fire.'

Livy (59 BC–AD 17) *History of Rome*

Paul Jamin 1893

The start of a terrible revenge

Soon after the Senones had descended on Rome, ancient texts begin mentioning Celtic mercenaries as being involved in a whole range of Mediterranean conflicts. It seems that the Celts' Italian campaigns had been conducted with an exact foreknowledge of local conditions. Mercenary service was probably an early means by which they acquired such familiarity.

Many Transalpines, thirsting for action and spoils, went on to organize raids in Apulia, Campania and Etruria. In 385 BC Celts helped Dionysius I of Syracuse to reduce the Etruscans' power and to lead a campaign against the city of Caere (Cerveteri): their alliance with Dionysius lasted about thirty years. In 332 BC the Senones and Rome made peace. Then a fresh coalition was formed to break Rome's renewed expansion: the Senones, Etruscans, Umbrians and others made a league, but were finally defeated at Sentinum in Umbria in 295 BC.

Suppression then began. The Senones were conclusively beaten by Rome in 283 BC and their lands were redistributed. In 249 there was another crisis; the Boii (originally from Bohemia) appealed for help to the Transalpine Gauls, but together they were defeated in a terrible battle in 225 BC near Telamon in Etruria. This war finally ended in 222 BC after the Romans captured Mediolanum (Milan), capital of the Celtic Insubres. In 191 BC it was the turn of the Boii, and they submitted conclusively to Rome.

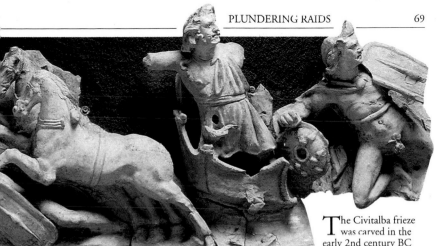

Boasting to Alexander the Great

The other direction into which the Celts, under Segovesus, had been sent by the birds of omen was central Europe and the Balkans. Bands of Celts probably reached Pannonia (Hungary) near the end of the 5th century BC: cemeteries like that at Stupava near Bratislava (Slovakia) produce characteristic objects, such as belt clasps, swords and knives. The main line of entry was the Danube.

A Celtic delegation, probably from Pannonia, met Alexander the Great in 335 BC somewhere near where the Morava flows into the Danube, and they exchanged pledges or diplomatic gifts. Alexander asked the delegates in passing what they most feared among men, hoping his own fame had reached Celtic lands to spread fear and respect. Their reply surprised him: that the Celts feared nothing except perhaps that the sky might fall in on them one day. Alexander called them friends, made them allies, and dismissed them, observing that they were braggarts.

The Waldalgesheim style

Contact with the Etruscans and Greeks became closer in the 4th century BC. Celtic artists – starting in Celto-Italic workshops –

The Civitalba frieze was carved in the early 2nd century BC to commemorate Rome's victory over the invading Celts. Above, in the centre, a Celt on his chariot knocks down one of his companions as he flees; behind him another defends himself from the pursuing Romans. Below: bust of Alexander the Great by Lysippus. Opposite: 3rd-century helmet from Çiumesti (Romania).

assimilated Mediterranean elements and went on to develop in a new direction, creating a flowing vegetal technique still called the Waldalgesheim style after jewelry of this type from a rich Rhineland grave. It is based on foliage and palmettes worked into continuous chains in repetitive compositions in which static and dynamic elements alternate. At times vegetal motifs seem to transform fleetingly into human faces.

In the Eigenbilzen tomb (Limbourg) a drinking-horn had a decorative openwork mount (above): the strip of palmettes and floral motifs are typical of the flowing vegetal style.

Of Celtic remains in Italy, the most southerly find so far is a ceremonial helmet (p. 64) with this type of decoration from Canosa di Puglia (Bari). The golden torque from Santa Paolina di Filottrano (Ancona), in one of the cemeteries of the Senonian Marches, illustrates this typically Celtic integration of Mediterranean motifs, as does a silver fibula from Bern-Schosshalde (Switzerland). For the new style quickly spread north of the Alps and even into the west of France, where finds of ceremonial helmets show this was a period of general Celtic expansion. An iron helmet from Agris (Charente), plated in bronze that is itself completely covered in

pure gold, is a masterpiece typical of 4th-century
Celtic goldsmithing (opposite below).

The Cisalpine Celts kept a firm hold on trade
in coral, treasure of the Tyrrhenian Sea, especially
from the Bay of Naples. This trade began in the
6th century BC and now increased, linked with
the production of torques, helmets and sword
scabbards.

The Danubian look

Techniques of Mediterranean and Black Sea
inspiration merged in the 3rd century BC in a
mannered taste for jewelry covered in pseudo-filigree
and knobbly protrusions. Virtuosity in casting bronze
reached an exceptionally high level and the fully
modelled style flourished.

New types of personal ornament appeared, such as
women's chain belts made with heavy, finely worked
links and enamelled pendants. Cast bracelets,
and ankle rings with hollow clasps and oval
bosses, were all the rage in the Danube
area, Bohemia and Germany. These
led on to rings decorated with
baroque reliefs and spirals,
sometimes arranged
in triangles or
tribrachs from
which human
faces projected;
some reached the south-west of Gaul.

At a time when Celtic warriors were confronting
the Hellenistic world, Hungary was the source of a
new type of art on sword scabbards. This spread west
to Switzerland, across Gaul and into Britain, and
eastwards into the Balkans. The basic new theme
was two imaginary animals face to face – such as
dragons, bipeds with erect tail or penis, or spindly
birds. These magical motifs were sometimes inlaid
or plated in gold, and shifted subtly between plant
and animal shapes.

Terret ring with
human head from
the Paris area. It is very
like examples found on
routes taken by the
Celts' long-range
expeditions, such as at
Mezek (Bulgaria). Their
design, sometimes in the
form of tribrachs, shows
a human head emerging
from spiral designs in
relief.

A late 3rd-century BC
bronze fibula from
Slovenia (left) is treated
in pseudo-filigree. This
was an effect obtained
by casting rather than
by applying very fine
threads that were
positioned individually.
This style of decoration
was adopted by the
western Celts and
appears again on some
jewelry in Champagne.

The dome of the
helmet (opposite)
from Agris (Charente)
carries palmette designs
and has coral studs fixed
in place with silver
rivets. Coral inlays also
decorate the cheek-piece
on which beaded
threads form flowers and
a ram-headed snake.

On to pastures new

The Macedonian empire stood
in the way of Celtic expansion
for a long time. In the 4th
century BC the Celts occupied
north-western Hungary, south-
western Slovakia and part of
Transylvania. When Alexander the
Great died in 323 BC, they moved
on. The conflicts that riddled the
Hellenistic world after his death
offered employment for mercenaries,
all the more welcome to the Celts because the
situation in Italy was beginning to turn sour.
Transalpines in search of adventure were now turning
to the Atlantic, but even more to the Balkans.

The shoe was a theme much prized by the Celts. Here in the form of a 3rd-century BC Hungarian vase, it also crops up on fibulae, especially at Hallein in Austria.

The eastward thrust came to a head with the
famous expedition into Greece and assault on Apollo's
sanctuary at Delphi. At the beginning of the 3rd
century BC an initial invasion of Thrace ended in
failure. The major onslaught then came in 280 BC
when three separate groups attacked in concert.
Thrace and the lands of the Triballi were invaded
by Celts under Cerethrius; Illyria and Macedonia
by Bolgios' warriors; and Paeonia by troops under
Brennus and Acichorius. The Celts probably entered
Macedonia along the Morava Valley, and inflicted
a bitter defeat upon Ptolemy Ceraunus' army; he
himself was captured and beheaded.

The gold of Delphi

After this victory the Celtic army split in two.
Brennus took advantage of the opening ahead and
swept into Greece, his southward march was
interrupted by battles and he suffered heavy losses
of men. After passing through Thermopylae with
his élite troops, he launched a raid on Delphi in
279 BC, the notoriety of which reached epic
proportions. It was a disaster. One legend relates
that Apollo himself wrought a miracle to avert

Apollo, in the legend, appeared with a crash at the crucial moment when the barbarians were about to plunder his temple's treasure. The Celts undoubtedly coveted Delphi's gold, though could they have carried off the thousands of kilograms discovered much later by the Romans in sanctuaries around Toulouse? The same event as seen by a Gallo-Roman potter (below) and by a 19th-century painter (right).

sacrilege; another says that Delphi was sacked and its treasures carried off into Gaul. Brennus himself was killed. Another detachment of Celts that remained in Thrace was defeated in 277 BC and turned back into Bulgaria, where they founded the short-lived kingdom of Tylis.

Thus ended the great invasion of Greece. Groups of armed men drifted around and took service as mercenaries. Campaigns that lasted only a few years have not left many archaeological traces, but there are

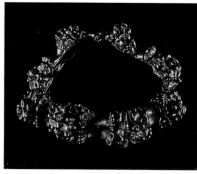

enough to confirm the identity of invaders from the Danube area.

Eastern Celts and Galatians

The relationship between the Celts and the great barbarian peoples around the Black Sea was of a very different sort. There may perhaps have been trading contact, especially along the Danube. Certain shared cultural features, like the custom of head-hunting which was also practised by

After killing his wife, a Gaul kills himself: this statue was part of a group dedicated in Pergamum by Attalus I in the late 3rd century BC. After his victory over the Galatians in *c.* 230 BC Attalus I, known as Soter (Saviour), took the title King of Pergamum.

the Scordisci, or appreciable influences in the decoration of luxury items, prove that ideas were exchanged and goods circulated: a torque from Cibar Varos is the earliest Celtic object from Thrace.

One group of Celts, the Galatians who crossed into Asia Minor, did try to fit into the Hellenic world. A section of Brennus' army joined up with Nicomedes I of Bithynia, who settled them in an area between his own kingdom and that of Antiochus I of Syria. This settlement only brought trouble to western Anatolia and provoked constant hostilities. The Galatians were driven back towards the high plateaux, the poorest area of Asia Minor,

A recent study connected with restoration of *The Dying Gaul* (below), sometimes called *The Capitoline Gaul*, a late 3rd-century BC statue, has questioned the traditional view that it was only a marble copy of a bronze original made for the sanctuary at Pergamum. In fact the marble, which comes from Asia Minor, and its superb artistry now suggest that this is after all the original work.

where they terrorized the large towns in the neighbourhood, including Gordium and Midas. They meddled in the affairs of the local Hellenic states around 240 BC and even attacked Pergamum, but Attalus I defeated them several times. Strongly Hellenized and far from their original homes, they eventually formed an isolated enclave that is said by ancient writers to have preserved its Celtic language and traditions into the Christian era.

Crossing the Pyrenees

In south-western France, where there was clearly defined settlement by Aquitanian peoples in the 5th century BC, archaeological evidence reveals

Far left: the fine gold of the bracelet from Lasgraïsses (Tarn) is said to have come from the treasure of Delphi carried off by the Tectosages (a people from Toulouse, some of whom also settled in northern Galatia). It is a sample of Celtic goldworking dating from the 3rd and 2nd centuries BC. Jewelry in this florid sculptural style has been very occasionally found in the former Yugoslavia.

Celtic infiltration from the East: chariot burials as far as the confines of Poitou, and a scattering of typically Celtic fibulae into the heart of the Pyrenees. This influence was sporadic until the 3rd century BC, when a new culture emerged. The sites of Vieille-Toulouse and Agen were Celtic strongholds, and the gold torques from Tarn and Haute-Garonne confirm their arrival.

Found in the River Tarn, France, this late 3rd-century BC bracelet (left) bears an unmistakable likeness to those made by the eastern Celts, from whom it may perhaps have been imported.

The presence of Celts in the Iberian peninsula is proved by a combination of ancient texts, linguistics and place-names. Celtiberians occupied the central regions of the peninsula, and other areas were also affected: in Lusitania (Portugal) traces of an archaic Celtic dialect have turned up. The Celts seem to have arrived in Galicia, a Gallic area, in the mid-1st century BC. It was therefore Celticized very late, but defended sites and hoards of torques were increasing in numbers there from 500 BC onwards. Could this have been a reaction to the arrival of the first Celtic settlers? Massive 'Celtiberic' sculptures have come from these *castros*; they portray wild boars, bulls and hieratic warriors holding a shield and wearing a torque.

A Celtiberian warrior? In Portugal, the stone statue from Castro do Lezenho (below), dating from the 2nd or 1st century BC, portrays a man whose torque (and shield) resemble Celtic statuary.

Armorica

Throughout the Bronze Age all the Atlantic regions of Europe shared a

common culture and economy. Occupied by people from the same ethnic stock, these areas are rich in natural resources, especially in tin, whose fame had reached the Mediterranean world and attracted many explorers. Armorica entered the Celtic sphere between the 5th and 4th centuries BC: fragments of wine flagons and weapons found in the cemetery at Tronoën (Finistère) and gold beads from a souterrain (underground chamber) at Tréglonou (Finistère) suggest regular contact with Celts further inland, although a strong regional distinctiveness still remained. Armorican Breton, the only Celtic language still spoken in continental Europe, is the best surviving evidence that the area did belong to what was once a vast Celtic province. The very fine local pottery long continued to be inspired by metal wares from northern Italy.

In the 4th century BC Breton pottery was strongly influenced by Italo-Celtic bronze vessels with stamped decoration. Curvilinear decoration on this pottery vase (above left) from a barrow at Kervenez (Finistère) suggests inspiration by the vegetal style.

A bronze dagger sheath (above right) from Kernavest (Morbihan) returns in the 5th century BC to stamped decoration, widely used in the 6th century on the collars and belts of the first Celtic princes.

The Roman military eagle spread its wings across the Alps. Soon Caesar was threatening Gaul. Consternation spread among the Celtic tribes, who gathered together behind Vercingetorix. The defeat at Alesia signalled the demise of Celtic Europe. In Britain and Ireland the vanquished barbarians were to lay down the remnants of their ancient culture.

CHAPTER 4

THE CELTS AGAINST THE MIGHT OF ROME

The Romans went into battle (left) wearing breastplates with metal parts and disciplined in fighting methods by former campaigns. Bare-chested and reckless, the Celts met them protected only by helmets and shields. Symbol of power and magical charm, some of their swords and daggers were given an anthropomorphic hilt, with a human head between brackets that suggest stylized arms and legs (right).

Early in the 2nd century BC the Roman conquest and assimilation of Cisalpine Gaul was completed. After seventy years of resistance the Iberian peninsula submitted in 133 BC. The task of connecting Italy by land with the new Spanish provinces now began.

The conquest of Narbonensis

On the south coast of Gaul Rome had a loyal ally in Massilia (the Latin form of Massalia, now Marseilles), a city that was having difficulty in protecting its sea-trade from attacks by Ligurian pirates and in defending itself on land from the troublesome Gauls. Massilia made a first appeal for help from Rome in 154 BC, and the Ligurian tribes that were besieging its colonies around Nice and Antibes were repulsed by force of arms. When the conflict was settled, Rome withdrew. A generation later, in 125 BC, Massilia made a new appeal for help against the Celto-Ligurian Salluvii, who were defeated in 124. The Romans took their oppidum at Entremont. But the most powerful Gaulish people on the left bank of the Rhone, the Allobroges, gave refuge to the Salluvii. In 122 a fresh Roman army headed against them, and despite the intervention of Bituitus, king of the Arverni, crossed the Alps and was victorious.

The hegemony that the Arverni claimed to hold over Gaul forced the Romans to move in. Bituitus

In Narbonensis, a mixed area conquered by Rome in 121 BC, towns soon bore a Greco-Roman stamp. Neighbouring peoples, apart from the Ligurians in the south, were Celtic: Volcae in the west and Allobroges in the north-east, close to the Aedui. Above left is a present-day view of Glanum, a small town with lively trade destroyed by the Romans in 125 BC, then rebuilt and active during the Gallo-Roman period.

gathered 300,000 men to meet them, but the battle ended in disaster for the Gauls. Rome was able to set up the province of Gallia Narbonensis, or Provincia (Provence), on annexed territory along the

Having beaten the Romans in Noricum, the fearsome Germanic Cimbri were finally defeated at Vercelli in Piedmont (engraving left), where they were crushed by Marius' army in 101 BC.

Trade routes with the south ended at Massilia, and the conquest of Narbonensis intensified their use. Between 75 and 60 BC a ship 40 m long sank near Hyères (Var) with its cargo (below and left). It is the largest ancient wreck found off the French coast. Excavation started in 1972, and it proved to contain 6000 amphorae of Italian wine arranged in three layers, as well as crates of pottery vessels.

Mediterranean coast between Italy and the Pyrenees; the port of Narbo (Narbonne) became its capital.

A twofold danger: Germania and Rome

In the east, another threat was looming: the invasions of the Cimbri and Teutones, which lasted from 113 to 101 BC. The Cimbri came from the shores of the North Sea and Jutland, while the Teutones, originally from the Baltic coastline, had perhaps already settled permanently around the Main. The Cimbri were driven back from Bavaria and Bohemia by the Celtic

tribe of the Boii. They reached the Celtic state of Noricum to the east of the Alps and then headed for Italy. The Romans were unable to halt their advance until 101 BC, when Gaul emerged from the ordeal worn out and in disarray.

The Suevi, another Germanic people, reached Alsace in around 70 BC. In c. 61 or 60 BC their ferocious king, Ariovistus, inflicted a severe defeat upon a Gallic army. Another enemy arose in south-eastern Europe: the Dacians under their king Burebista overwhelmed the Celtic populations of the Danube basin. Around 60 BC the Dacians in Austria made an alliance with Ariovistus, who had already united other tribes from central and northern Germany. Faced with imminent danger, the Gallic Aedui appealed for Roman support; other Celtic peoples reacted differently.

The dramatic migration of the Helvetii

Under this mounting threat, the Helvetii, described by the contemporary Greek historian Posidonius as 'rich in gold but a peaceful people', decided in 58 BC to leave Switzerland for south-western France, in one of the last great Celtic migrations. Originally from the east, probably from the Black Forest, they had started moving fifty years earlier to flee the Germanic advance.

Thousands now left their villages, setting them alight, and assembled at the tip of Lake Geneva. Near Genava, a strategically placed Allobrogan oppidum, many other neighbouring peoples came to join them. Numbers rose to 368,000, of whom 92,000 were fighting men. They planned to cross the Rhone by the Genava bridge and follow the river south into friendly territory.

Julius Caesar (102–44 BC), governor of the Roman province, heard of their project, went to Genava and cut the bridge. Attempts

Called in to help the Aedui, Caesar drove the Suevi from Alsace in 58 BC. Left: he meets Ariovistus, king of the Suevi.

A large oak figure (opposite below), dated *c.* 80 BC and supposedly a protective deity, was retrieved from the port of Geneva. Discovery of a similar statue has suggested the function of enormous torques like that in the 'St Louis' treasure from Basel (below left). Hollow and with large terminals, these objects once had an iron core coated in resin and clay, thus limiting the amount of gold used while giving an impression of mass.

The Helvetii lit the ramparts of Mont Vully (below) with torches in 58 BC before leaving for Geneva.

at negotiation failed. The Helvetii then tried to move north through Sequanian territory with their 2800 ox-carts, but were attacked and massacred in Aeduan territory by the Roman legions. Divico, their chief, asked for a truce. Caesar demanded hostages. Divico replied that the Helvetii were accustomed to take, not give, hostages, and war was renewed. A rumour went about that the Roman legions were retreating towards Bibracte. But the Helvetian offensive became a rout, and in the end they surrendered. Caesar ordered the survivors to go back to their abandoned lands and rebuild their houses.

Bridging the Rhine (below left), a crucial feat in 55 BC, was intended to allow Caesar to press on to the east.

OSISMII

CORIOSOLIT

REDON

VENETI

NAMNET

The struggle for independence

Once called in for help against the Germani, Caesar never looked back. He now had a foothold in Gaul, and needed to secure his political position in Rome. Without provocation he mounted a campaign against the Belgae, the most powerful people in Gaul: some, like the Remi, alarmed by the unexpected attack, surrendered. Others assembled an army, but were defeated on the Aisne and pushed back to the Somme.

At the same time, Caesar, who had come under heavy attack by the Nervii in the north, also sent legions to Armorica to subjugate the maritime peoples, decimate their fleet and isolate central Gaul.

Gaul was not homogeneous at the time of the conquest: there were the Belgae in the north, the Armoricans in the west, and the so-called Gauls in the centre, where a zone of Arvernian influence and a central-eastern zone can be distinguished. In the south was Narbonensis, only part of which was Celtic. The south-west was essentially Aquitanian, despite several Celtic enclaves around Bordeaux and Agen. The Parisii occupied an area between the Belgae, Armoricans and Gauls.

PI

BITUR
VIVI

T

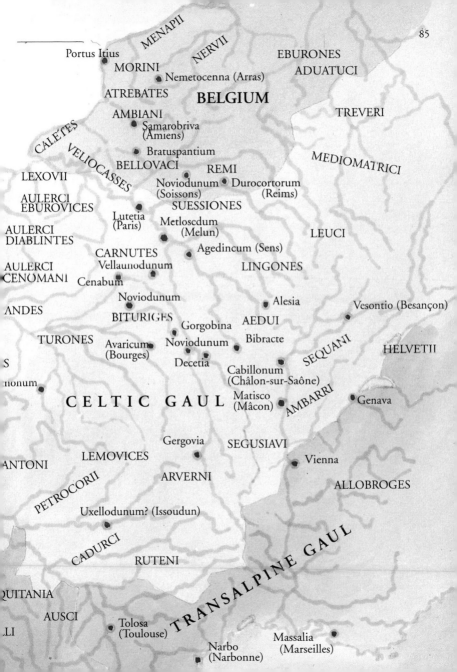

MENAPII

Portus Itius

NERVII

MORINI

EBURONES

ADUATUCI

Nemetocenna (Arras)

ATREBATES

BELGIUM

TREVERI

AMBIANI

Samarobriva
(Amiens)

CALETES

Bratuspantium

MEDIOMATRICI

VELIOCASSES

BELLOVACI

REMI

LEXOVII

Noviodunum
(Soissons)

Durocortorum
(Reims)

AULERCI
EBUROVICES

SUESSIONES

AULERCI
DIABLINTES

Lutetia
(Paris)

Metloscdum
(Melun)

LEUCI

CARNUTES

Agedincum (Sens)

AULERCI
CENOMANI

Vellaunodunum

LINGONES

Cenabum

ANDES

Noviodunum

Alesia

Vesontio (Besançon)

BITURIGES

Gorgobina

AEDUI

TURONES

Avaricum
(Bourges)

Noviodunum

Bibracte

SEQUANI

HELVETII

S

Decetia

Cabillonum
(Châlon-sur-Saône)

nonum

CELTIC GAUL

Matisco
(Mâcon)

AMBARRI

Genava

Gergovia

SEGUSIAVI

ANTONI

LEMOVICES

Vienna

PETROCORII

ARVERNI

ALLOBROGES

Uxellodunum? (Issoudun)

CADURCI

RUTENI

TRANSALPINE GAUL

QUITANIA

AUSCI

Tolosa
(Toulouse)

Massalia
(Marseilles)

LI

Narbo
(Narbonne)

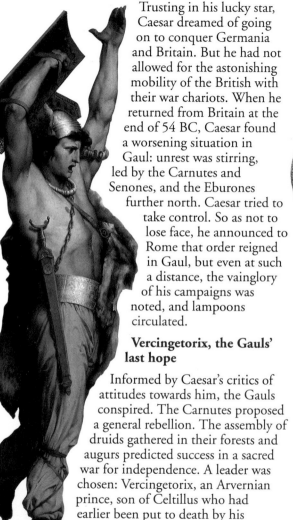

Trusting in his lucky star, Caesar dreamed of going on to conquer Germania and Britain. But he had not allowed for the astonishing mobility of the British with their war chariots. When he returned from Britain at the end of 54 BC, Caesar found a worsening situation in Gaul: unrest was stirring, led by the Carnutes and Senones, and the Eburones further north. Caesar tried to take control. So as not to lose face, he announced to Rome that order reigned in Gaul, but even at such a distance, the vainglory of his campaigns was noted, and lampoons circulated.

Vercingetorix, the Gauls' last hope

Informed by Caesar's critics of attitudes towards him, the Gauls conspired. The Carnutes proposed a general rebellion. The assembly of druids gathered in their forests and augurs predicted success in a sacred war for independence. A leader was chosen: Vercingetorix, an Arvernian prince, son of Celtillus who had earlier been put to death by his compatriots for attempting to reinstate the kingship. Still in his youth, Vercingetorix had been with Caesar's army

From Auvergne, a gold coin of 52 BC in Vercingetorix's name (below) has an idealized portrait of the young chief. Twenty-seven of these coins are known to exist.

Like many 19th-century painted or sculpted portraits of warriors, this painting, *Vercingetorix Summons the Gauls to the Defence of Alesia*, by François Ehrmann (detail, left) is inspired not by conquest-period equipment but by anachronistic objects at least half a millennium older, probably because of the more advanced state of Early Iron Age excavations at the time. The arm ring, the belt of stamped sheet bronze and the antenna sword all date from around 600 BC; the helmet, older still, is a type from the Italian late Bronze Age. The torque is the only Late Iron Age accessory.

among the Gallic contingents sent by various peoples as proof of their allegiance.

As soon as he was elected leader of the Gallic resistance, he set about winning over the majority of central Gaul and Armorica and organizing Gaul as a whole for the great uprising. He had detailed plans

This silver coin (left) of *c.* 50 BC, minted by the Aedui, is in the name of their chief Dubnorex (Dumnorix). The reverse here shows a triumphant figure holding the head of a vanquished enemy in one hand and a carnyx (a sort of war-horn) and wild-boar emblem in the other. Dumnorix, initially Caesar's ally, finally rallied to the cause of his compatriots.

to cut the Roman army's lines of communication between Italy and Gaul by launching a simultaneous offensive against Gallia Narbonensis, the Aedui and Caesar's legions en route for the Saône. But Caesar's speed thwarted his plans. Provincia had had time to prepare its defence and Vercingetorix had to turn back into Arvernian territory.

The Bituriges were unwilling to sacrifice Avaricum (Bourges) by implementing the scorched-earth policy advocated by Vercingetorix. Despite a heroic stand, the town was taken and 40,000 of its inhabitants perished. This disaster taught the Gauls a lesson, and Vercingetorix's authority came out of it reinforced.

The Romans laid effective siege works before Avaricum (left), capital town of the Bituriges, which finally fell in 52 BC.

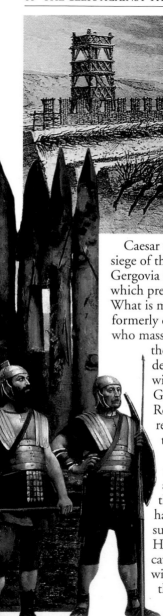

Caesar then embarked upon the siege of the chief Arvernian citadel Gergovia (near Clermont-Ferrand), which presented great difficulties. What is more, he was betrayed by his formerly constant allies the Aedui, who massacred all the Romans in their territory. Thwarted, he decided to return to Provincia with his armies. Just when the Gauls were about to chase the Romans from their lands, a reckless escapade reversed their fortunes.

Vercingetorix, who had remained in the rear with all his infantry, let loose three of his cavalry corps to harass the Romans and make sure that they departed. Heady with victory, the cavalry swore not to return without twice passing through the enemy column. They had forgotten that

Sketch of Alesia (above) made on the orders of Napoleon III. Here, on Mont Auxois, on the border between the Lingones and the Aedui, Vercingetorix took refuge in 52 BC. The Roman army besieged it, encircling the town with two lines of defence doubled by ditches and a third outside line directed against the army of relief. Between the two ditches a whole network of spikes was arranged, while holes dug in the earth allowed the movements of the Gauls to be closely monitored.

Germanic auxiliaries had come to Caesar's aid, and that the Roman army never let itself be taken by surprise. The Roman troops turned around and pursued the Gallic cavalry back to Vercingetorix's camp. Shattered, the Gauls took refuge in Alesia (Côte-d'Or), citadel of the Mandubii.

Gaul's last hours of liberty

Vercingetorix sent his cavalry back with the task of raising men from every tribe and state for a final contest. He shut himself in Alesia, with 80,000 high-ranking warriors and enough supplies for thirty days, awaiting reinforcements from all of Gaul. Around the citadel the Romans constructed a network of lines of defence that neither the besieged warriors nor the reinforcements managed to cross. Vercingetorix's orders were not well understood, and the general levy was late. When at last help arrived, the besieged men were at the end of their strength. Several battles took place, but without any real strategic co-ordination. The Gallic forces were routed and the various contingents fled, each returning to their own communities. For Vercingetorix this meant abandonment, defeat and despair. During the following months Caesar was absorbed in using force to quell the lingering resistance of the Bituriges, Carnutes and Bellovaci. In Poitou, Limousin, and Cahors he also met desperate last stands. But Gaul had finally fallen. So Celtic Europe suffered unstable conditions and its territory was greatly reduced during the 1st century BC. After taking Gaul, the Romans occupied Pannonia in 12 BC.

The classic scene of Vercingetorix's surrender took place between centurions guarding the gates of the Roman camp (below and opposite). Mounted on his horse, Vercingetorix galloped across the space between the two camps. He rode a circle to the right around the tribunal, as though magically to bind his conqueror, then cast his arms without a word at the startled proconsul's feet. If Caesar only gave a dry account of Vercingetorix's sacrifice, the nobility of his deed was raised to legendary status by historians from Livy to Plutarch and Dio Cassius, especially as he enabled many of his companions to flee (above left) by distracting the Romans' attention.

Having at first copied staters (below right) of Philip of Macedon (359–36 BC), Celtic die engravers gave free rein to their creativity. On the obverse, heads sprouted shocks of curly hair. On the reverse, the conventional horse team gave way to fantasy (such as a horse with a giant bird above or a human-headed horse). The first issues were fairly heavy coins of pure metal. Some peoples, such as the Parisii, had gold staters until the conquest. Others used triple alloys of copper, gold and silver, or progressively debased silver coins, or even, like the Cenomani, kept a surface appearance of gold by plating over a base alloy. Outside their own area, coins were

only worth the weight of noble metal they contained, a fact that explains the occurrence of the little balances often found on settlements.

Then in
Bohemia and
Moravia the
Germani wiped
out a Celtic
civilization already
radically altered by
the Dacians.

The British Isles

There is evidence in Britain
of the first arrivals of Celts
from the Continent in the
5th century BC. Equipment
very similar to that in
Champagne at the same
period has been found:
daggers with decorated
sheaths and fibulae made by

craftsmen from the Marne region. It seems likely that groups from Belgic Gaul Celticized the British Isles. Two Insular peoples bear the names of continental Belgic tribes: the Parisii (from around Paris) in Yorkshire and the Atrebates (from around Arras) south of the Thames in Hampshire and Sussex. Commius, king of the Atrebates, who assisted Caesar from 55 to 54 BC, later became one of the leaders of the anti-Roman Gallic coalition and ended up taking refuge in Britain.

B oudicca, queen of the Iceni of East Anglia, killed herself in AD 61 after a failed rebellion against the Romans.

These Insular populations successfully opposed Caesar's ambitions with their armies of chariots. Claudius' legions finally embarked upon conquest in AD 43, but British resistance continued for some time. In AD 61 a rebellion led by Boudicca, queen of the Iceni, attacked the towns of Camulodunum (Colchester) and Londinium (London) and massacred entire Roman garrisons, but it was in the end suppressed. By AD 77 most of Britain had been brought under Roman rule, apart from the Welsh mountains and the north of Scotland; Ireland was untouched and would always remain profoundly Celtic.

In Ireland, whose rulers occupied fortified dwellings but where oppida were unknown, writing was to be a late development, allegedly introduced by St Patrick in AD 432 along with Christianity. Irish literature bears witness to its Celtic inheritance. The Irish poets finally committed an oral tradition going back to the bards to the written – manuscript – page.

T he numerous promontory forts on the Irish coastline may date from the Celtic Iron Age. Opposite above: the dry-stone ramparts of Oghil, Ireland, dated between the 1st and 5th centuries AD.

T he early 1st-century AD horned bronze helmet (left) found near Waterloo Bridge in London was put in the river as a votive offering. A very rare specimen, its striking appearance has led to its being widely used in popular images of the Gauls. Some headdresses from Ireland with two or three bronze horns may be sacred crowns.

From Brittany to Britain

In Brittany the small geometric motifs stamped upon pottery vessels are also found on such prestigious weapons as the dagger from Kernavest (Morbihan) or the helmet from Tronoën (Finistère). Some carved granite standing stones allow links to be made with Insular art: a 4th-century BC stone at Trégastel (Côtes-d'Armor) or the Kermaria stone at Pont-l'Abbé (Finistère) with its decorated geometric panels seem to derive from the same source of inspiration as five standing stones in Ireland dated between the 3rd and 1st centuries BC.

There is little evidence for Celtic art in the British Isles before the 4th or even 3rd centuries BC, and it was only in the 2nd century BC that British art attained a fully accomplished style, traces of which are found on weapons such as sword scabbards and large shields. In the 1st century BC two currents became clear, one characterized by stylized human or animal elements, and the other by a whole series of abstract shapes and patterns governed by the use of compasses. Art on mirror backs illustrates the climax of this refined technique. While on the Continent the conventions of Greco-Roman art gradually imposed a leaning towards sobriety, a so-called 'severe' style, the Celtic tradition remained firmly rooted in Britain for a long time, even after its partial conquest.

Found in the Thames, the Battersea shield was never used for combat. Its symmetrical design, glass inlay and interlacing are peculiar to British Celtic art of the 1st century AD.

Making bronze mirrors with sumptuously worked backs was a speciality of workshops in southern England between the 1st century BC and the 1st century AD. Above the openwork handle spread a sophisticated pattern that framed plain smooth areas in grooved basketwork motifs.

In Ireland, remote from Roman influence, Celtic culture stayed intact, and Late Iron-Age art merged imperceptibly into Christian art. Small bronze objects – boxes, pins or bridle bits – perpetuated Celtic decorative motifs. There are bronze discs whose use is still a mystery. Irish jewelry in the early Middle Ages, especially

Enigmatic carved stones may be relics of an ancient sacred knowledge of the universe. Irish stones are usually three or four centuries more recent than Armorican examples. A squat pyramid from Kermaria (Finistère) of the 4th century BC (left) has a different design on each of its four faces. The rounded Turoe stone (far left) from Galway (1st century BC) has vegetal motifs exactly like much older continental jewelry.

penannular brooches and trimmings, still bore designs of Iron-Age inspiration: heads of water birds, curvilinear patterns, tribrachs and S-shapes. This Celtic taste for decorative virtuosity was to continue in the art of manuscript illumination.

The oppida, fortified towns

The first Celtic towns, protected by a rampart known as *murus gallicus,* developed almost everywhere in Gaul. Urban life took shape with specialized quarters laid out along streets: craftsmen's houses, buildings of various sorts with religious functions and assembly places. A sort of bourgeoisie that produced and consumed semi-luxury goods and held political power emerged. A central oppidum served as capital of a region, where coinage was struck and exchanged. The proliferation of coinage types reveals the subdivision of territories and the increasing autonomy of small political units.

The network of land and river communications was extending fast. Mass-produced craft goods (like fibulae) and imported Mediterranean products (such as wine and oil) came into general use and betray the growing influence of the Roman world nearby.

Part of the population must have lived on the proceeds of trade, but it is not known whether craftsmen were free, independent or attached to the noble or equestrian class. One of the functions of

At the highest point in Bibracte, a sanctuary overlooked the homes of noble Aedui; craftsmen's quarters and market places were on the outskirts. An enameller's workshop was found next to a bronzesmith's, with crucibles, colouring matter, iron tongs and scraps from workings. Bibracte is the only oppidum to have yielded so much evidence for glassworking.

Rings (above right) from Mathay (Doubs) in violet (manganese), green (copper), blue (cobalt), with yellow spiral decoration (lead), or even transparent, prove that Celtic glassworkers knew how to handle oxides.

The Aeduan capital, Bibracte (left), on Mont Beuvray (Nièvre), was an important oppidum, 135 hectares in extent. Vercingetorix was given his command there by the assembly of Gaulish chiefs, and it was there, after the battle of Alesia, that Caesar took up winter quarters and began to write his commentaries on the Gallic war.

these fortified towns was to protect strategic points in this fragile economy, by serving as stopping places, centres of attraction on the main communication routes and refuges for the local population. But who governed the oppida – kings, princes or an aristocracy? It seems that the situation differed from one region to another, though power in general seems to have fallen into the hands of merchant nobles.

The *murus gallicus* (reconstruction below) is a peculiarly Celtic type of rampart. It has a wooden framework of intersecting beams whose rows are separated by layers of earth or rubble. Long iron nails pinned the beams at each intersection. It was given a cladding of large blocks of close-fitting stone through which the ends of the beams protruded.

The blacksmith held a privileged position among craftsmen. Huge numbers of iron tools and weapons were being made from the 2nd century BC onwards: such things as axes, swords, spearheads, parts of shields and the chains that attached sword scabbards to the belt; and jewelry, including plenty of brooches. The power of the aristocracy was based on its possession of iron, used not only for the production of arms and armour, but also for all the agricultural equipment that was needed to till the land. On the far left, on an iron sword blade of *c.* 100 BC, is an oval stamp with a pair of goats confronting each other, probably the armourer's mark. His name, Korisios, is also inscribed in Greek letters. This is one of the oldest examples of writing north of the Alps.

The abundance of natural wealth

In the countryside quarries began to be exploited: for clay for pottery, marl to spread on fields and stone for building or sculpture. Even if the intensive use of naturally abundant woodland led to excessive

The Gallic site of Villeneuve-St-Germain (left) was an oppidum lying just above water level, almost surrounded by a meander of the Aisne and barred to the south by a rampart. Intensively occupied after the Roman conquest, from 50 to 15 BC, it is typical of built-up settlements at the end of independence, with long thatched buildings separated by occasional gaps. Recent excavations have revealed where coins were made, where bronzesmiths, blacksmiths, carpenters and furriers worked, and have also produced remains of glass beads and little wheels.

deforestation, the Gauls were discriminating in the use they made of wood. They were responsible for inventing the barrel, and excelled in the manufacture of chariots.

The indigenous farm was the essential setting for all kinds of agricultural activities, which developed and flourished in a green and hospitable countryside

Iron knives and sheep-shears from La Tène (Switzerland) dating from the 3rd or 2nd century BC.

scattered with woods and sources of water. Hunting only provided for a small part of the diet; most animals needed for food or for draught were domesticated. Pigs, cattle, sheep, goats, horses, donkeys and dogs were all smaller than today's breeds.

Thanks to an impressive iron industry, there was a full range of agricultural equipment by the 1st century BC, identical to that being used by peasants until the beginning of the 20th century. In some areas fields were manured and enriched. Alongside the swing plough, there was a wheeled plough to improve yields. The scythe and sickle were sometimes replaced by an animal-drawn reaping machine called a *vallus*. Villages multiplied, especially on the plains, with thatched wooden houses, grain-storage pits and enclosed animal pasture. Some isolated and defended farms were also aristocratic households, like that at Paule (Côtes-d'Armor).

In experimental farms such as the one near Quin in Ireland (top), studies over many years allow Celtic farming, stock-raising, building and craft techniques to be rediscovered.

To improve firing, kilns with two separate chambers (above) had a combustion chamber below and a space above where unfired pots were placed, sometimes in large quantities.

There are terrifying ancient accounts of Celtic groves inhabited by the gods: the wind never blew on the trees, birds were frightened to perch on their branches and the world was filled with icy shadows that the sun never pierced. Monuments and religious practices reveal the complexity of the Celtic mind. Despite the cruel demands of their gods, the Celts remained confident of the soul's immortality.

CHAPTER 5
REALMS OF RELIGION

A sheet-bronze statue 70 cm high of a warrior-god (right) was recently found in the sanctuary at St-Maur-en-Chaussée (Oise). It contains a lot of zinc, like some coins of the 1st century AD. Hexagonal pieces similar to his shield were also found deposited as offerings. His symmetrical hairstyle in thick strands resembles stone statues from the South of France, especially the 2nd-century BC capital with severed heads (opposite) from the Entremont sanctuary (Bouches-du-Rhône), where the styles of classical Italy and the Celto-Ligurians merged.

Celtic sanctuaries were essentially sacred spaces cut off from the rest of the world. Sometimes simply natural places like a mountain, lake, confluence or clearing, they can also be identified by architectural features, though little usually survives apart from the faint marks of post-holes where wooden structures once stood. Archaeologists have distinguished four types of sanctuary: *Viereckschanzen* or quadrangular enclosures; sanctuaries of Belgic or Picardy type, best known around Beauvais and Amiens; the Celto-Ligurian sanctuaries of the South of France; and sacred springs.

Mysterious *Viereckschanzen*

These places, with their square shape, as their German name indicates, and bounded by one or more ditches or a bank of earth, normally contain almost nothing apart from scraps of pottery, and are found from central France to Bohemia and Moravia. They have been particularly well studied in southern Germany, where they seem to have been used from the 4th to the

Ritual pits were dug by the Celts from the 4th century BC onwards in sanctuaries like the *Viereckschanzen.* The custom of consigning the remains of burials and various offerings, animal bones, pottery and metal or wooden objects to the depths of the earth continued into the Gallo-Roman period, as the funerary pits bear witness at Vieille-Toulouse or (left and opposite) Bernard-en-Vendée, where more than twenty have been found since 1858.

This wooden statue of a stag was found at the bottom of a 2nd-century BC pit at Fellbach-Schmiden in Baden-Württemberg, along with various other animals rearing up on their hind legs. They probably formed part of a symmetrical carving.

1st centuries BC; every year aerial photography discovers more of them. The complex arrangements inside these enclosures seem to follow no general pattern. Only the smallest of them (*c.* 60 m wide) have structural remains in the central area reserved for ceremonies. Ritual shafts have sometimes been dug there.

Belgic theatres for macabre ceremonies

Some of the so-called Belgic or Picardy enclosures, used between the 3rd and 1st centuries BC, have produced many ritual offerings. These sites measure 30 to 50 m along each side, are surrounded by ditches and a bank topped by a palisade, and have at the centre a wooden temple open to the east that was originally decorated with paintings or sculptures and had walls laden with prestigious displays of warriors' weapons. Texts by Caesar and the historian Livy (59 BC–AD 17) suggest that in some temples war trophies were hung up by victorious tribes and might remain on the sanctuary walls for several decades, until they fell down: it seems they were then smashed and thrown into the enclosure pit.

Rendered unusable, these bent swords from the Belgic sanctuary at Gournay-sur-Aronde (Oise), like many examples from 3rd-century BC graves, are loaded with symbolic meaning. It is generally thought that they have been 'killed', as if to share their owners' death.

At Gournay-sur-Aronde (Oise), the sanctuary inside the oppidum has yielded iron weapons and animal bones, the relics of numerous sacrifices scattered into its boundary ditches. Its entrance, carefully arranged at a gap in the ditch, consisted of a porch surmounted by trophies that included human skulls with their empty and terrifying stare.

Stacks of bones

Animal sacrifice took different forms according to the animal, the season and the divinity being honoured. Oxen were commonest, especially old animals, but also plenty of bulls, killed by axe blows to the poll or forehead. The whole carcass was put into the great pit in the temple and left until the bones fell apart. The skull was then displayed with warrior offerings and the rest were thrown into the ditch. Horses were also sacrificed. Sheep and pigs were reserved for consumption at the ritual feasts held on the site.

Human bones also performed ritual functions. One of the largest rural sanctuaries in Gaul was built in the 3rd century BC at Ribemont-sur-Ancre (Somme) – 800 m long, with a complex layout. Here, long bones from about 1000 individuals aged fifteen to twenty years were stacked and criss-crossed into

Domesticated horses first appeared in Gaul during the Bronze Age, and were about the size of large ponies today. Caesar tells of the Gauls' great passion for horses, and of how they even imported larger breeds. The high value accorded to horses was reflected in unusual ways of dealing with them when they died. They were neither eaten nor merely dumped, but carefully buried in pits.

Very distinctive funerary rites and traces of sacrifice have come to light at a site at Ribemont-sur-Ancre (Somme). An earthen bank marked the edge of an open ditch where headless and dismembered corpses of men and women must have been placed over a period of several decades at the end of the 3rd century BC. About 1000 young subjects with no apparent symptoms of disease were probably sacrificed. Their arm and leg bones, collected around a central post into which weapons and horses' bones were fitted, formed a strange cubic monument measuring 1.60 m each way.

a sinister cubic monument measuring
1.60 m each way. Community ossuaries
made pillar-like structures at the four
inside corners of the enclosure.
Between each of these bone pillars,
dismembered bodies littered the
ground; their skulls had been
detached and treated. How these
people died remains a mystery.

The hero cult

The 2nd-century BC grammarian
and poet Nicander of Colophon
noted that the Celts practised
divination at the tombs of their
dead warriors, where they would
spend the night. In the South of
France, a whole range of stone
sculptures found in sanctuaries
reveals the development of the
ancient hero cult, already
widespread in the 6th century BC, as the
Hirschlanden stele (p. 29) suggests.

Entremont, Roquepertuse and Glanum in
Provence are among the best known of these
Celto-Ligurian sanctuaries linked to oppida on the
fringe of the Celtic world. Here, stone pillars with
niches to take human skulls, decorated lintels and

painted sculptures of gods, warriors in breastplates or sitting cross-legged and animals (birds or monsters), were originally part of an architectural complex. The sanctuary at Entremont was a long building shaped like a portico, with square columns that once supported a roof. That at Roquepertuse, built on two terraces and in full use during the 3rd century BC, was burnt down in the 2nd century BC,

With half-closed eyes sunk in their sockets, long hair and puckered mouth, the Entremont 'severed head' (far left) has an open hand resting upon it. This gesture might commemorate a victor taking possession of a vanquished enemy's remains. The most famous statue from the same sanctuary (centre), 70 cm tall, is of a squatting warrior wearing a breastplate. Left: detail of a pillar carved with two stylized heads. Whether these monuments at Entremont were made before or after the conquest remains undecided.

when Roman influence was increasing. No sacrificial remains have been found, nor typical ritual structures such as an altar or pit. The presence of exposed human skulls is a point of similarity with the Belgic sanctuaries, but the statuary suggests that here they were dedicated to glorious heroes or ancestors.

Also in Bouches-du-Rhône, the Roquepertuse sanctuary was a place on a small hill where the Salluvii held religious gatherings before the Romans destroyed it. Statues of warrior-heroes and severed heads set in pillar niches (left) suggest distinctively Celtic rites, although the general cultural tone was Mediterranean.

Head hunters?

The head occupied a special place in Celtic art and religion. A severed head with half-closed eyes, sometimes without a mouth, and carved in stone, is a common theme at sanctuaries in the South of France. Sometimes the hero grasped a head by the hair or rested a hand on it. Was he recalling his warrior exploits? Or is the head meant to symbolize his own death?

A valid explanation has yet to be found for the human skulls displayed at these sanctuaries. Were they select victims from within the tribe? Or the severed heads of enemies? There certainly were accounts of how after battles Celtic warriors would turn to collecting heads: they would hang the heads of enemies they had killed across their horses' necks and later nail them up as trophies on the doors of their houses. They would preserve the heads of distinguished chiefs in cedar oil and show them off with pride to strangers.

In all events, the Celto-Ligurian sanctuaries clearly suggest that their demanding and pitiless religion had a bloodthirsty fascination with deified warrior-heroes.

Divine water

'Copious water falls from dark springs ... and grim, shapeless images of gods are rough-hewn from tree trunks, rotten with age, whose eerie pallor is chilling.' So said the Roman poet Lucan (39–65 AD), adding that none but the priest dared approach this grove near Marseilles, which was given over to the gods. Springs, ponds, caves, wells and lakes were repositories of sacrificial gold and were actually privileged sacred places: the springs at Chamalières (Puy-de-Dôme) and the headwaters of the Seine served as sanctuaries where hundreds of carved wooden votive offerings, jewelry and coins were deposited, mostly after the Roman conquest.

The Gallo-Romans were in fact only continuing a cult that went back to the Bronze Age and was widely practised by the Celts. The site at La Tène on Lake Neuchâtel in Switzerland was probably one of these vast open-air sanctuaries that reappeared when the water level was low at the end of the 19th

century. Near a small village two bridges which crossed the River Thielle in antiquity were offering-points for hundreds of iron weapons, especially swords; personal ornaments were rare by comparison.

Many human skeletons bore traces of wounds, which tends to rule out the suggestion that they died a natural death. Skulls of cattle and horses were specially selected in preference to long bones.

Jewelry offerings

Precious goods collected as votive offerings, especially hoards with golden torques, reflect a ritual practised across the whole of Celtic Europe, especially between the 4th and 1st centuries BC. The Erstfeld hoard (Uri canton), abandoned in an Alpine pass in the heart of Switzerland, typifies these sacrifices to nature: here, golden torques and bracelets decorated with mythological figures were consecrated to a mountain deity. In Bohemia the Duchcov hoard, found

Wooden statues placed as votive offerings from the source of the Seine in the 1st century BC (opposite) were cloaked like pilgrims in a typically Gaulish hooded cape or wore the traditional torque (left). Opposite below: a 1st-century BC miniature boat in gold with movable mast and oars from the Broighter treasure (Northern Ireland). Among other bronzes from Neuvy-en Sullias (Loiret), including animals and a male figurine, a naked dancing-girl skims the floor with all the grace of her 13 cm (left). This freedom of style dates the piece to the late 1st century BC, while the rest of the hoard seems to have been buried in the 3rd century AD.

in a spring, like the Lauterach hoard from Austria, contained large quantities of women's jewelry, especially fibulae. Concentrations of hoards have come to light around Toulouse in south-western France and in parts of southern and eastern England. Eight hoards were buried close to one another at Snettisham in Norfolk. One found in 1990 had 35 kg of precious metal, mostly base alloys of copper, gold and silver.

Coinage and religion

The first Celtic gold coinage from the 4th and especially the 3rd centuries BC was included in votive offerings and is often found associated with torques, for instance at Tayac (Gironde), Niederzier (Rhineland) and Snettisham (Norfolk). Scraps of mythology can be gleaned from coins. Some designs, full of meaning, contain surprising elements, especially on Armorican coins: human heads with a line coming out of the crown or forehead, chains of dots ending in little floating heads, contorted figures, heads with monstrous eyes or human-headed horses in fantastic harness.

Some of the very earliest Celtic gold coins, issued in an area between

A sacred shrub from the oppidum of Manching (Bavaria): this branch made of plated wood has side-shoots bearing bronze ivy-leaves plated thinly in gold. This cult object suggesting the sacred tree was carefully hidden in a wooden chest in the 3rd or 2nd century BC.

southern Germany and Switzerland, and especially by the tribes of the Boii, were convex and decorated with magical designs (three globules or a torque with spherical ends), and were amassed in votive hoards. They tended to resurface after heavy rain, to the amazement of 18th-century peasants, who dubbed them 'rainbow cups', imagining a link between these simultaneous apparitions.

Secret divinities

The Celts practised nature cults devoted to the sky, stars, earth, hills, mountains, forests and clearings (even particular trees), rivers, lakes, the sea and animals symbolic of strength. A poem dating from the end of the 3rd century BC and quoted in the *Greek Anthology* mentions the 'jealous Rhine' to which the Celts would appeal for a verdict on the legitimacy of their offspring, while a Gallic chief, victorious in northern Italy, boasted of being the son of the Rhine. Names also hint at these cults: such as tribal ones – the Eburones were the Yews and the Tarbelli the Bulls – or personal ones, like Brannogenos, Son of the Crow, or Matugenos, Son of the Bear.

Brennus is said to have burst out laughing when he was told about the temple of Delphi and of how the Greeks believed the gods had human forms that they depicted in wood and stone. The Celts themselves were generally reluctant to make images of their gods. Though this situation may have been due to the influence of the druids, jealous guardians of contact with the gods, it also reflects an age-old taste for abstraction. However, after the Roman conquest, divine images quickly became very widespread. Later on, the legendary tales of the Insular Celts teem with allusions to images of deities as they must have existed on the Continent.

• Rainbow cups• (left), plentiful in southern Germany in the 3rd century BC, were probably more of magical than of economic value. Torques, groups of dots and other decorative motifs composed a sacred grammar.

The name of the deity (below) from Euffigneix (Haute-Marne), a late 1st-century BC limestone pillar-statue found in a pit, is not known. Its resemblance to a wooden sculpture suggests that this figure, wearing the torque symbolic of divinity, was probably often carved in wood.

ESVS.

Portraits of bloodthirsty gods

Some Gallic peoples are said to have appeased cruel Teutates and terrible Esus with hideous sacrifices. These seem to have been fearsome gods, with a thirst for human blood. Medieval texts relate the sacrifices they were offered according to their tastes. For Teutates, a man was drowned in a tub; for Esus, a man was hung from a tree and pulled to pieces; while for Taranis, several were burnt alive in a hollow tree.

Caesar, in his *Gallic War*, gives a list of deities worshipped by his enemies. He describes them by their Roman names: Mercury, inventor of the arts and protector of highways and trade, Apollo who cures illnesses, Minerva, Jupiter and so on.

Speaking of Mars, he adds that when a war began the Celts would dedicate to him all the booty they might win, and that, having won, they would kill the living spoils and heap up the rest in a sacred place. Piles of miscellaneous booty could be seen in many communities, and it was very unusual for anyone to dare, for fear of the religious law, either to withhold his own takings or to lay a sacrilegious hand upon the

Carved stones from the *Nautes Parisiacae* monument were found in 1711 under the Cathedral of Notre-Dame in Paris, having been re-used in a late Imperial wall. One block bears a dedication to Jupiter made in Tiberius' reign by this guild of Gallo-Roman watermen. Another represents a god on each of its four faces: Jupiter, Vulcan, Esus and Tarvos Trigaranus. The face with Esus (top left) is the only definite image known of this god.

offerings: such crimes would be punished with a terrible death. There was the same divine hierarchy in Ireland.

Lug, surnamed *Samildánach* and armed with javelin and sling, was god of all the arts. The Dagda, the good god, a fighter armed with a big club and lord of abundance with his inexhaustible cauldron, was surnamed Ollathair, father of all. Ogma symbolized physical strength, Dian Cécht was the physician god, and Goibniu the divine smith. The Welsh gods had the same functions but different names.

Shared beliefs

Apparent regional diversity conceals an underlying unity in Celtic mythology. The triad is a recurrent symbol.

It has recently emerged that the Roquepertuse limestone statues were once covered in painted decoration. This sculpture (left), among the most important from southern Gaul, shows two heads with different faces joined back to back like some Greek images of Hermes, and treated very realistically. It is a clear example of the influence of Hellenistic art on a society that had been steeped in Mediterranean culture for a long time.

A Gallo-Roman bronze statuette *c.* 20 cm high of Artio, goddess with a bear, was found at Muri near Bern (Switzerland). She has sometimes been regarded as a remote ancestor of the town's own emblem. Bears and wolves must have been plentiful in Celtic times, but few traces of them remain apart from a few teeth in graves in the Ardennes.

The cauldron found at Gundestrup (Denmark) in 1891 had been dismantled and deposited as a votive offering in a bog. It was probably made in the Balkans, on the eastern fringe of the Celtic world, a lot of whose mythology it brings together. Made of partially gilded silver, it is 69 cm in diameter and dates from the 1st century BC. On the outside are seven panels bearing heads of more or less terrifying divinities. The inside displays ritual scenes, in particular a whole procession, complete with musicians and sacrificial ceremonies. Cernunnos (top left) is represented sitting cross-legged, with a ram-headed snake (symbol of earthly prosperity and aggressive force) in one hand and in the other a twisted torque of the same type that he himself is wearing round his neck. A helmeted female divinity (bottom left) is surrounded by exotic animals – a cat, elephants and winged griffins – a very un-Celtic collection in which influence from the Black Sea is felt.

TARVOS TRIGARANVS

There is evidence of deep concern for the earth, sacred geography, frontiers and natural configurations. Every distinctive feature of the landscape had a mythical significance.

The cult of Mercury covered vast areas of Europe. His indigenous name, Lug, recurs in about fifteen ancient place-names, including Lugdunum (now Lyons) and Luguvalium (now Carlisle). The great harvest festival of Lugnasad was celebrated in all Celtic areas.

The goddesses Rosmerta, Nantosuelta, Damona, Sirona, Nemetona and many others were partners of male divinities. It is not always easy to tell them apart from the *matres* or *matronae*, divine mothers whose cult was deeply rooted in Celtic religious tradition. As mothers of the peoples they carried horns of plenty, baskets of fruit and fertility symbols. The father god Dispater was great lord of the earth, and the Gauls claimed to be his descendants.

The cult of a divine smith corresponding to Vulcan is known by his Insular name Goibniu in Ireland or Gofannon in Wales. Esus, a good god, though avid for human blood, is shown as a labourer and associated with Tarvos Trigaranus, the bull with three cranes. The bull was symbol of fertility and fighting strength. The stag, another fighting male, was the most prestigious wild animal: his antlers grow afresh every year, a symbol of nature's cycle.

The druids

Forming a privileged intellectual élite, masters of literature and poetry, the druids devoted about twenty years to their training, memorizing sacred texts. They were forbidden to write these down,

CERNVNNOS.

Tarvos Trigaranus, the bull with three cranes (top left), may be echoed in Irish epics: the hero Cú Chulainn pursued a divine bull, which was alerted by three goddesses in the form of crows. Cernunnos (above), the supreme god of Celtic forests, often appears wearing a torque; here bracelets hang from his antlers.

though by Caesar's time the druids were literate. They were versed in mathematics, studied the movements of the stars and claimed they could measure the universe. Mediators between mankind and the gods, to whom they alone had access, they regulated religious ceremonies, presided at sacrifices and interpreted omens. They taught that the soul does not perish after death but moves from one body to another, or goes on living 'elsewhere'. This belief fostered courage and helped overcome the fear of death. In popular imagery, druids are often shown harvesting mistletoe. This was not only a magic ritual but an expression of deeper beliefs and worship of a great Celtic god connected with the natural cycle of the seasons. Mistletoe, a perennial plant, was to the tree what the soul was to the body, proceeding from the god, or even the god himself incarnate as a plant.

❛ The druids ... consider nothing more sacred than mistletoe and the tree that it grows on, so long as it is an oak.... Below the tree they prepare a sacrifice and religious feast, and bring two white bulls whose horns are bound for the first time. A priest clad in white climbs the tree, cuts the mistletoe with a golden hook and catches it on a white cloak. Victims are sacrificed with prayers to the god to render this offering propitious....❜

Pliny the Elder
(AD 23–79)
Natural History, XVI.95

bɤeneɤaɕɪo

The valiant barbarians of the Iron Age gave way before the combined onslaught of the Germani and Rome. Nonetheless, throughout the first millennium AD, Celtic traditions were being worked into the background of early Christian art. It was especially in areas like Ireland and northern Scotland, which never came under Roman rule, that Celtic aesthetic styles flourished.

CHAPTER 6
CELTIC MEMORIES

The Book of Kells, a masterpiece of Insular Celtic art created in *c.* 800 AD, contains the Latin Gospels accompanied by Irish texts. The Chi-Rho page (left) has details so fine that they are barely visible to the naked eye. Right: statuette of a deity clasping a lyre from Paule (Côtes-d'Armor), made *c.* 70 BC.

Celtic society went on evolving throughout its history, while its geographical organization also changed. In Caesar's time Gaul was organized on the basis of a network of urban oppida, and each political grouping achieved stability through the institutions that were shared amongst its component tribal units. In pre-Christian Ireland, by contrast, tribal groups were widely scattered in small units around a rural landscape, and the king was the crucial symbol of unity and of the bond with ancestral territory. The family, clan and kingdom, ties of blood and the collective ownership of land were the organizing principles of a society that had become archaic compared with continental models.

Christianity arrived in Ireland in the 5th century, spread by the famous missions of St Patrick. Latin learning awakened interest in ancient culture and the monasteries began to amass wealth and power. Ancient Celtic styles were reborn in Christian iconography and inspired manuscript illumination. Monumental carved stone crosses, reliquaries, shrines and croziers, Celtic art in which a Viking influence can sometimes be detected, were still being made in the 12th century. It was only after the Anglo-Norman invasion of 1169 and the arrival of new monastic orders from the Continent that Celtic art was supplanted by other models. Only in literature were its remnants preserved.

Old Irish language and legends

The first written texts go back to the 6th century AD. These are short, mainly funerary inscriptions engraved in ogham (writing based on the Latin alphabet but shaped as lines or dashes). Later on, glosses inserted into 7th- to 9th-century Latin manuscripts allowed Old Irish to be identified and its grammar to be defined.

The Book of Durrow (*c.* 675 AD, left) was written in the monastery at Durrow, reputedly by St Columba himself. It contains four Latin Gospels with translation and commentary. Its decoration drew upon a goldworking tradition that survived until the 12th century and also influenced the style of Irish crosses (opposite), with a circle around the central motif that was to disappear with Romanesque art. Below: in solid gold and silver, the Irish Tara brooch (8th century AD) perfectly illustrates Insular Celtic artists' *horror vacui*, or dread of empty spaces.

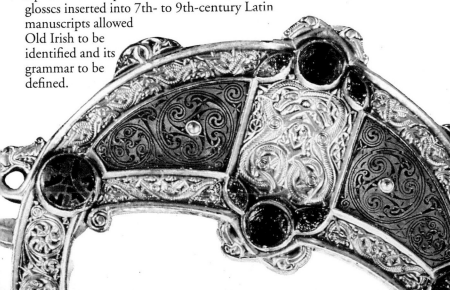

A gloss in tiny script was added in the 12th century to an 8th-century Irish manuscript (left). It is a legal text on the rights of women.

It appears in books like the Life of St Columba, the Book of Kells and the Book of Armagh.

Legal texts written in Old Irish give an impression of the concepts and procedures in force in Ireland in the 7th and 8th centuries AD. Welsh laws survive from the 10th century.

Traditional tales were transcribed very early in Ireland. Poetry appeared in the 6th century and narrative prose at the end of the 7th century. The exploits of heroes, legendary kings and mythical figures were told in cycles: their conception and birth, then their expeditions to the Otherworld, amorous

The huge white horse carved into the hillside at Uffington (Oxfordshire), near an Iron-Age hillfort, remains one of the great riddles of archaeology since its design can only be seen clearly from the air. Normally ascribed to an early Celtic period, it may not have been made until the Middle Ages.

adventures, battles and finally their exemplary death. This heroic ideal corresponded closely to that of the continental Iron Age.

The heroes of Irish epic

One of the most famous works is the Ulster Cycle whose hero, Cú Chulainn, was son of a divinity and died young but covered in glory. He did not care, he

Harpists were highly esteemed in Celtic society. Warriors gladly drew inspiration from the songs of poets who extolled their exploits. These epic tales

said, if he only lived a day and a night, so long as the tale of his exploits lived for ever. He had a magic power that could rouse him to a frenzy. After killing many enemies, he went into a trance and was suffused with a radiance that was not to leave him until he died. To calm his frenzied mind, his people once presented him with a hundred naked women, but he did not even see them.

Another Irish cycle that also appeared in the 7th century had a profound influence upon European thought at the end of the Middle Ages – it is known as the Fenian Cycle. It draws on the Celtic tradition

spawned a tradition that has survived to this day: the songs of Ireland and Wales are still well known. Above: a 19th-century lithograph which reveals, with its freedom of interpretation, the Romantics' infatuation with the Celts.

of a band of warrior-huntsmen led by an extraordinary chief, Finn Mac Cumaill, who protected the kingdom from outside incursions. In Wales this theme was overlaid by the Arthurian legend, widely spread by oral tradition. This began to take shape in the 6th century, fuelled by endless tales of wars with the Angles. The cauldron of plenty, supernatural objects, the heroes and their adventures are all Celtic themes.

The legacy of the Celts

Celtic languages declined during the Roman period, but they never actually stopped being spoken. Cornish disappeared in the 18th century, but modern Welsh, Armorican Breton, Irish and Scottish Gaelic are very much alive today, and being taught. Few traces of ancient Celtic survive in English apart from words such as breeches (Gaulish *bracae*) or bard (Gaulish *bardos*). Celtic elements are common in place-names: the Rhine relates to Celtic *renos* (raging flow) and Irish *rian* (sea), and place-names in -combe (coomb) to *cumba* (a vase) or Welsh *cwm* (valley).

Celtic literary themes bridge the centuries. The Arthurian Cycle left a particularly rich legacy: King Arthur became a British national hero; in the

Popular 19th-century image and 1973 cinema version: the wicker man conjures up the ancient Celts' cruel rites.

12th century the Normans took him to Sicily and Chrétien de Troyes set his deeds to verse; even Dante invoked Arthur's furious blow as he struck the traitor, 'piercing his chest and shadow at one blow' (*Inferno*, canto XXXII). In the 18th century Macpherson had resounding success with *The Works of Ossian*, a bard who supposedly lived in the 3rd century AD, and certainly enthused the pre-Romantics.

Through music, songs and popular dances, story-telling and ceilidhs, Celtic traditions are still kept alive today and reinterpreted in an imaginative and vivid way.

In this 19th-century painting, *Ossian Receives the Souls of Heroes who Died for Their Country*, by Anne-Louis Girodet-Trioson, Napoleon Bonaparte enters into legend as a living hero. Overleaf: detail of a 4th-century wine flagon handle join from the tomb of the Waldalgesheim princess (Rhineland).

DOCUMENTS

From Strabo's descriptions to accounts
of the Celts' resistance to Rome:
a few fragments of
what was once a civilization.

Celtic territory on the map of the ancient world

The early Greeks called them 'Keltoi', the Romans 'Galli'; they were also called 'Galatai'. But they all came from the same ethnic group, whose territory fluctuated with different conquests and retreats.

STRABON.

The earliest written allusions to the Celts described their homelands, always presented as dark, uninviting and mysterious in the eye of Greek poets or Carthaginian explorers. At first both scholars and poets located them vaguely to the west or north of the Mediterranean.

By the 8th century BC Homer had already mentioned western areas and their populations in the Odyssey.

We reached the deep-flowing ocean where the Cimmerians have their lands and their town. This people is hidden under clouds, in mists which the sun's bright rays have never pierced ... a dismal night hangs over these unfortunates.

Homer (*c.* 9th century BC)
Odyssey, XI.13–9

The land of the Hyperboreans

Legends of the Delphic sanctuary recounted that soon after his birth Apollo visited the Hyperboreans – a mythical people of the savage north – in a chariot drawn by swans. They located this place 'beyond the mountains, in lands of legend, where no compass points the way'.

Hesiod, an 8th- or 7th-century BC Greek poet from Boeotia referred to a river in the west as the 'Eridanus with deep eddies', conceivably the Rhone. In his account of Hercules' voyage from the Isles of the Hesperides to Greece he alluded to what was later to become Gaul.

Aristeas, a mid 6th-century Greek poet, is said to have written an epic on the Arimaspeans in which he mentioned the Hyperboreans, in the far north-west of Europe.

Beyond the Issedones live the one-eyed Arimaspeans; gold-guarding griffins live beyond them; and then the Hyperboreans stretch to the sea.

Aristeas (6th century)
Quoted by Herodotus
Histories, IV.13

A century later, the great Greek poet Pindar described the Hyperboreans as an ancient, sacred people, immune from illness, old age, fatigue and war. There was, however, little exact knowledge of northern Europe in Greece at that time.

It was through ignorance of these [northern] regions that people invented the mythical Rhipaean Mountains and the Hyperboreans....

Strabo (64 BC–AD 21)
Geography, VII.3.1

First mention of the Celts

Celtic lands were clearly named in the 6th century BC by the Greek historian and geographer Hecataeus of Miletus, who was born c. 548 BC at Miletus in Asia Minor and died c. 475. He himself travelled west of Greece. He drew up a map of inhabited territory and described a sort of world tour, with a commentary on his map.

As for Herodotus, the vast area that he specified in the 5th century BC between the sources of the Danube (southern Germany) and the Iberic (Spanish) peninsula is the area occupied by the Celts, as present-day archaeology confirms.

The river Ister rises among the Celts and the town of Pyrene and crosses the whole of Europe. And the Celts are beyond the Pillars of Hercules, next to the Cynetes, who live furthest west of all the peoples of Europe.

Herodotus (*c.* 480–25 BC)
History, II.33

He had probably encountered the Celts, whose name he mentions in connection with a trip he made to the shores of the Black Sea.

An offshore view of Celtic territory

The notion that Celts inhabited western Europe is due to accounts by seafarers who often only described coastal regions.

Himilco, an early 5th-century BC Carthaginian navigator instructed to reconnoitre the Atlantic coastline and the seas of northern Europe, gave terrifying descriptions of these places, which were later reworked by the Latin poet Avienus.

Were these patent exaggerations of the dangers that he faced sincere or were they to conceal the failure of his mission? Or were they intended to sow confusion about the trade route for tin which Himilco was supposed to investigate?

He said he took all of four months to cross the ocean from the Pillars of Hercules to the Oestrymnides (Armorican or British islands) 'on a sea that was sluggish and blocked with weed, in danger on shoals and surrounded by sea monsters'. He said that west of the Pillars of Hercules the absence of wind and a perpetual fog always made navigation impossible.

Pytheas was another navigator and an astronomer, a 4th-century BC Massaliote of Greek origin who explored the Atlantic and the North Sea. He certainly reached the Baltic Sea and left an astonishing account of his ocean travels.

A Greek geographer of the conquest period

With Strabo, born in Cappadocia in 64 BC, we get our first exact geographical description of Celtic territory. In his time, in the early 1st century AD, it only reached from the Rhine to the British Isles.

After Iberia, we come to Celtic territory, which reaches eastwards as far as the Rhine. Its entire northern edge is bathed by the British Channel, since the whole length of Britain runs parallel to and opposite Celtica for a distance of 5000 stades. The eastern boundary of Celtica is defined by the river Rhine, which runs parallel to the Pyrenees. Its southern boundary is partly formed by the Alps, at the point where they start to rise close to the Rhine, and partly by the Mediterranean Sea at the point that is called the Galatic gulf, where there are the famous cities of Massalia [Marseilles] and Narbo [Narbonne].

In his *Geography* Strabo locates the territories of the western barbarians between the northern Alps, the British Isles and the Iberian peninsula. A. Berthelot's map (below) was drawn in 1933 from Strabo's descriptions.

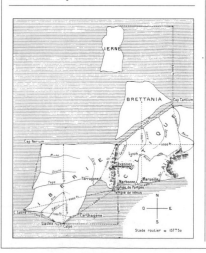

Opposite this gulf, but facing the other way, there is another gulf that is also called the Galatic gulf, but faces north and towards Britain. Here, Celtic territory reaches its narrowest point, for it forms an isthmus of less than 3000 but more than 2000 stades. Between [these two gulfs] there is a mountain ridge that runs at right-angles to the Pyrenees, called Mount Cemmenos [the Cévennes, i.e. the Massif Central]; this comes to an end in the midst of the plains of Celtica. The Alps, which are very high mountains, describe a curve whose convex side faces the same plains of Celtica and Mount Cemmenos, while its hollow side faces Ligurian territory and Italy.

Strabo (64 BC–AD 21)
Geography, II.5.28

Beyond the Pillars of Hercules

Inspired by reading accounts of their travels by Himilco and Pytheas, a Latin poet, Rufus Festus Avienus, worked their images of a wild and dangerous west into his own geographical poem Ora Maritima.

Water washes into open land and the world is completely surrounded by it. The Atlantic gulf lies at the point where the deep sea leaves the ocean and opens out to form the Mediterranean. Here stand the town of Gades [Gadir], once called Tartessus, and the pillars of dogged Hercules, Abyla and Calpe: Calpe on the left and Abyla close to Libya; the fierce north wind rages against them, but they stand firm.

Here, too, the head of a promontory [Brittany] juts out, called Oestrymnis in a bygone age. Most of the towering mass of its rocky summit faces into the warm south wind. Under this promontory's crest the Oestrymnian gulf spreads out ... and contains the Oestrymnides, islands with broad plains and rich mines of tin and lead. The people here are powerful, proud, energetic and industrious, trading in everything. Their boats sail freely on this rough expanse of sea and the ocean teeming with monsters. They do not make hulls of pitch pine, nor do they shape wooden keels in the usual way; but, amazingly, they contrive their ships by stitching skins together, and cross the open sea on leather.

It takes a boat two days from there to reach the Sacred Isle, so called by the ancients. This island [Ireland] in the midst of the sea is very large, mostly inhabited by Hibernian folk. Nearby, back in the opposite direction, is the island of the Albiones [Britain].

From the Oestrymnides, if boats dare venture into waters where the northern skies ice the breeze, they reach Ligurian land, now deserted because the Celts have repeatedly driven its people away. The exiled Ligurians, driven by fate as so often happens, ended up where they now are, in places bristling with scrub, with stony soil, steep rocks and looming mountains thrusting skywards. For a long time the fugitives scratched a living from rock shelters, shunning the sea which they feared because of the ancient danger; then peace, leisure and security made them more daring and encouraged them to descend from their high dwellings to the seaboard.

Rufus Festus Avienus (4th century)
Ora Maritima, 80–112, 130–45

A present-day archaeologist's view

A contemporary specialist on the Celtic world, Alain Duval describes the extent of its territory at the height of its expansion. He places the various peoples where Caesar was later to encounter them.

The 3rd century BC marked the peak of Celtic expansion. The Celts then occupied a vast area stretching from the British Isles to the northern reaches of the Black Sea. Two great regions can be distinguished within it: a western Celtic zone and an eastern Celtic zone. The latter, in contact with the Hellenistic world (and not simply through the raids that armed bands launched into Greece) but also in contact with eastern neighbours like the Dacians, is by far the richer and more dynamic of the two. In the western Celtic zone, the tribes that Caesar later mentioned took up their positions in the 3rd and early 2nd centuries BC. Some of these tribes represent what can already rightfully be called Gauls, and as a result France is referred to as Gaul. In the north of Gaul and in England lived the Belgae (the Insular Belgae were called Britons). In the west of Gaul, the Gauls called themselves Armoricans. In the 2nd century BC some of the most powerful peoples of Gaul were the Senones, the Arverni of Auvergne, and the inhabitants of the vast region from Burgundy to the Swiss plateau, the Aedui and the Sequano-Helvetii. In Languedoc lived the Volcae. It is still not known whether they were part of the Arverni people or eastern Celts who migrated to Gaul.

Alain Duval
L'Art celtique de la Gaule, 1989

Classic portraits of early 'European Man'

'The Celts have a cool, damp, white and hairless skin like the Germani, Thracians and Scythians,' wrote the Greek physician Galen in the 2nd century AD. He also claimed, 'The Celts do not have a perfectly proportioned body'.

Although they can in no way be regarded as a race, the Celts have been attributed over the centuries with certain shared physical features or character traits, sometimes in stark contrast with the models that emerge from their own statues or from studying their skeletons.

An exaggeratedly Nordic type?

Classical writers, neighbours and contemporaries of the Celts went into raptures about their white skins, their light coloured eyes and hair and their powerful muscles. For Mediterraneans these men from the north were a constant source of amazement, and confronted them with a dazzling display of gold and silver. This is how Virgil summed up their physical appearance, as portrayed on Aeneas' shield.

Their hair was of gold, their clothing was of gold and light stripes brightened their cloaks. Their milk-white necks had gold collars around them, a pair of Alpine spears glinted in each warrior's hands, and their bodies were protected by tall shields.

Virgil (70–19 BC)
Aeneid, VIII.659–62

The myth of the huge blonde

Did the classical peoples think of themselves as very small? At any rate the barbarians' great vitality impressed them. The 1st-century BC Greek historian Diodorus Siculus wrote a World History *in forty books, from its origins to the Gallic war, and left this vivid account of the Gauls.*

The Gauls are tall, with moist white flesh; their hair is not only naturally blond, but they also make artificial efforts to lighten its colour by washing it frequently in lime water. They pull it back from the top of the head to the nape of the neck.... Thanks to this treatment their hair thickens until it is just like a horse's mane. Some shave their beards, others let them grow moderately; nobles keep their cheeks clean shaven but let their moustaches grow long until they cover their mouths.... They wear amazing clothes: tunics dyed in every colour and trousers that they call *bracae* [breeches]. They pin striped cloaks on top of thick cloth in winter and light material in summer, decorated with small, densely packed, multi-coloured squares.

Diodorus Siculus (1st century BC)
World History, V.28, 30

Impetuous warriors

Strabo, the Greek historian and geographer from Asia, wrote a Geography *in seventeen books. His descriptions of Gaul and the Gauls are the most accurate after Caesar's.*

The whole nation that is nowadays called Gallic or Galatic is war-mad, and both high-spirited and quick for battle although otherwise simple and not uncouth. Because of this, if the Gauls are provoked they tend to rush into a battle all together, without concealment or forward planning. For anyone who wants to outwit them they are therefore easy to deal with, since it is enough to provoke them into a rage by any means at all, at any time and in any place. It will then be found that they are willing to risk everything they have with nothing to rely on other than their sheer physical strength and courage. If gentle persuasion is used, however, they will readily apply themselves to useful things such as education and the art of speaking. Their strength is due partly to their size – for they are large – and partly to their numbers.... In addition to their simplicity and exuberance the Gauls have a propensity for empty-headed boasting and have a passion for personal ornamentation. They wear a lot of gold: they put golden collars around their necks and bracelets on their arms and wrists, while dignitaries wear dyed or stained clothing that is spangled with gold. Their vanity therefore makes them unbearable in victory, while defeat plunges them into deepest despair. Their thoughtlessness is also accompanied by traits of barbarity and savagery, as is so often the case with the populations of the north.

Strabo (64 BC–AD 21)
Geography, IV.4.2, 5

The Celtic temperament

It may be asked ... what can be learnt of the spirit of the Celts, and here fortunately Classical authors are ... able to throw some considerable light.

'The whole nation ... is war-mad, and both high-spirited and quick for battle although otherwise simple and not uncouth.' These few words by Strabo perfectly express the impression gained of the Celts as a living people from all the written sources, and not least from the native Irish tradition. Strabo makes it clear that his description applied to the time of Celtic independence before Roman rule, and it is well to remember that he, as well as Diodorus Siculus, and other writers, make extensive use of earlier authors who had been able to make personal observations of Celtic life. Personal bravery, amounting to recklessness on the battlefield, and, at home, hospitality and a strict code of etiquette towards visitors, shows the Celtic householder as comparable to, if not a better person than, many of his more historical successors in the European countryside. Against the general impression of high spirits, if not excitability, and the impermanence of concerted action, there must be set the evidence for individual responsibility, and duties within a well-defined social system. The love of bright colours, adornment, praise and entertainment, feasting and quarrelling, all have remained European foibles when conditions have allowed, and none would be more natural than amongst a rustic people dwelling in the temperate regions of Europe.

T. G. E. Powell
The Celts, 1983

Arrian, a Greek who obtained Roman citizenship and compiled the works of the stoic philosopher Epictetus (born c. AD 60), presents a calm and sober synthesis.

The Gauls are tall and have a high opinion of themselves.

Arrian (*c.* AD 96–180)
Anabasis of Alexander, I.4.6

Roman mistrust

In a speech of 69 BC in defence of the government of Transalpine Gaul, Cicero warned the Romans to beware of the Gauls, whose behaviour had made them unworthy of trust.

These are the very people who once went to Pythian Apollo at Delphi, so far away from their homelands, in order to desecrate and plunder the whole world's oracle.

These same people – so religious, so scrupulous testifying here in court – besieged the Capitol.... Do you think they are humble and submissive here today, in their cloaks and breeches?... Look at them, cheerful and arrogant, pouring into the Forum with a threat on their lips, trying to frighten us with the noise of their barbaric language.... It would be a monstrous black mark and a disgrace upon this empire if news reached Gaul that Roman senators and *equites* had given a verdict to suit the whim of the Gauls, not because of the merits of their case but because they were intimidated by their threats.

Cicero (106–43 BC)
Pro M. Fonteio, 14.30, 33; 16.36

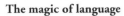

The magic of language

The oral tradition was crucial to Celtic culture, all the more so as it replaced writing. The art of speaking probably developed in as complex a way as the plastic arts, showing, like them, a taste for change.

In conversation, the Gauls' speech is brief and enigmatic, proceeding by allusions and innuendo and often exaggerating to puff themselves up and put others down. They have a threatening, boastful, tragic manner, and yet their minds are sharp and not without aptitude for learning.

Diodorus Siculus (1st century BC)
World History, V.31

The Celts love style, and their admiration for eloquence is unbounded. The Greek writer Lucian, who was travelling around Gaul during the second century BC, described a charming symbolic scene. An old man, clad in a lion skin, with a beaming smile, led a group of followers whose ears are attached to his tongue by thin gold and amber chains. They followed him eagerly, praised him and danced around him. The explanation that Lucian was given was that the old man, named Ogmios (an echo of the druidic Ogham), represented eloquence, for it grew with age, and was more powerful than brute strength, hence the lion-skin of Hercules.

John Sharkey
Celtic Mysteries: The Ancient Religion, 1975

Society and private life

Often rather biased, ancient accounts suggest a rough people with simple customs. The richness of archaeological evidence gives a wholly different impression of Celtic life, governed by laws, social structures and a relatively strict morality.

Caricature of the barbarian

Polybius, an admiring Greek historian of Roman affairs, visited Cisalpine Gaul himself. It seems, however, that the primitive culture he attributes to the Gauls – prefiguring Romantic versions – was no more than a device to conceal distinct gaps in his knowledge.

They lived in unwalled villages without much furniture to spare; for as they slept on beds of straw and leaves and fed on meat and spent their time exclusively on warfare and agriculture, their lives were simple, and they did not have any crafts or sciences. Each man's wealth took the form of cattle and gold, since only these things could be taken with them anywhere as they moved around and be shifted to suit their convenience. They held comradeship in highest esteem, since the most feared and powerful among them were those who were thought to have the most attendants and retainers.

Polybius (200–120 BC)
Histories, II.17

Social divisions

Caesar, a Roman proconsul linked by family ties with plebeian circles, described in detail in his Gallic War *not only his military campaigns of 58–1 BC but also his impressions of Gaul's inhabitants: an interesting mixture of precise observation and occasionally wild interpretation, demonstrating in eight books the saving aspect of the Roman army's intervention, for individuals, morals or civilization in general.*

In the whole of Gaul there are only two classes of men who count for anything and are considered, for the common people are like slaves: they can do nothing on their own account and are never consulted. Most of them, crushed either by debts and taxes or by the injustice of more powerful men, have handed themselves over into servitude to nobles who have assumed the same rights over them that masters have over slaves. The other two classes are the druids and the *equites* [knights or barons]. The former preside over religious matters, see to public and private sacrifices and expound doctrines ... [the latter are responsible for military affairs].

Caesar (102?–44 BC)
Gallic War, VI.13–5

The social order

The two main areas of the Celtic world significant in our enquiry into the druids, Gaul and Ireland, both provide evidence for the Celtic social order, which can be seen to have been essentially the same in both regions. The Irish vernacular sources show us a simpler and more rustic world than do the classical writers, particularly Caesar, describing Gaul, and this is consonant with the archaeological evidence for a higher degree of sophistication and technological achievement on the Continent. The major social units in Gaul were what are usually translated 'tribes' – *ethne* in the Greek and *civitates* in the Roman writers – and these have specific names, the familiar Helvetii or Veneti, Aedui or Atrebates. Within these large tribal areas there would be *pagi*, smaller territorial or kinship units or 'clans', and in Caesar's time there were impermanent and shifting political coalitions in which the more

powerful tribes might have several others in a relation of client powers. By this time too what had been an original system of tribal chieftainships (or 'kings') was being replaced by an annually elected magistracy in the Roman manner (a member of which was known as a *vergobretos*), or by the oligarchic rule of the council of elders originally responsible to the 'king' (*rix*) whose position had to some extent at least been elective from within the choice presented by the dynastic families, and there had also been a separate war leader on occasion. A phrase in Tacitus suggests that a similar decline in chieftainship had taken place in Britain.... Below the king and the royal family, society in Gaul was tripartite, with two classes of landowning freemen, the knights or barons (*equites*) from whom the council of elders was chosen, and the priesthood or clerisy, including *druides*. This learned class comprised not only druids, but bards (*bardoi*), and seers or diviners (*vates* or *manteis*), and probably other un-named functionaries. Below these representatives of church and state came the unfree and landless men, the *plebes*. There was an internal grading in power and position among the 'knights', and it seems that they did not constitute a closed caste, and some social mobility seems to have been possible. The druid and allied religious élite was equally not a caste, but open to entry from outside, from the class of *equites*.

The evidence from the law-tracts and hero-tales of Archaic Irish, which represent the earliest literary stratum, shows that the normal area of the tribe (*túath*) ruled by a 'king' (*ri*) was not comparable with the Gaulish *civitas*, but with the *pagus*. The nearest approach to *civitates* would have been the five sub-kingdoms or provinces (Ulster or Connacht for instance) each under a provincial 'king' and comprising a group of *túath* units: Ulster, to take an example, contained 35....

On a lower and more primitive scale, 'kingship' was universal in Ireland, elective from within the dynasty. Below the king came the landowning 'grades of nobility' – the Gaulish *equites* – and between them and the freemen commoners came those of exceptional gifts of skill, the *aes dána* or 'men of art'; expert craftsmen in things, word and thought, blacksmiths and bronze-workers, lawyers and genealogists, poets and musicians. In the Irish scheme of things druids designated as such are not normally in the dominant position the Gaulish (or at least Caesar's) evidence implies, but are contained within the men of art who were the men of learning, and also included the *filid* who were at once seers and wise men, and the repositories of the oral traditions not only of myth, legend, and family history, but of the formalized language and techniques of prosody in which these were preserved and transmitted, and the jurists responsible for customary law. There was a council of nobles, and a general assembly of the freemen of the tribe.... We see then a common pattern of society well documented in Gaul and Ireland, and by inference present elsewhere in the Celtic world.

Stuart Piggott
The Druids, 1975

Marriage, death and various cruelties

When men marry they receive a dowry from their brides, and to this they add a sum from their own possessions that is agreed as equivalent in value after an assessment; they keep a single account of this money and preserve all the interest on it. When one of them dies, the surviving spouse receives both portions together with the accumulated increase. Husbands have rights of life and death over their wives and children. Whenever a high-born head of family dies, his relatives assemble and, if there is anything suspicious about his death,

wives are interrogated like slaves. If found guilty, they are put to death by fire after every sort of cruel torment. By Gallic standards their funerals are magnificent and sumptuous; everything they think the dead man cherished in his lifetime is put on the pyre, even his animals; and also, not long before living memory, at properly conducted funerals the slaves and clients who had been dear to him were burnt along with him.

Caesar (102?–44 BC)
Gallic War, VI.19

Status of women

The women of the Gauls are not only like men in their stature but they are a match for them in courage as well.

Diodorus Siculus (lst century BC)
World History, V.32

It is generally assumed that the right of a wife to hold independent property, or of a daughter to inherit, is a late development appearing in parallel form in different Indo-European legal systems. On the other hand, a more liberal, but still common, practice seems to have been operative at very varying dates as illustrated in Aryan, Roman and Celtic legal custom. There is also the question of the very rich Celtic women's graves, as at Vix and Reinheim, to take but two recently discovered examples. Here women, buried singly, had been accorded the most splendid funerary chambers, and the most sumptuous adornment and accessories. Personal prestige and the right to possess property may account for such instances, while all the considerations taken together seem to suggest that incapacity of women was a reflection of primitive conditions, predominant in times of migration or hardship, though the legal system was always sufficiently elastic in periods of prosperity, from place to place, to permit greater female freedom in public and family interests.

T. G. F. Powell
The Celts, 1983

Homosexuality

Despite the fact that their wives are beautiful, the Celts have very little to do with them, but instead abandon themselves to a strange passion for other men. They usually sleep on the ground on skins of wild animals and tumble about with a bedfellow on either side. And what is strangest of all is that, without any thought for a natural sense of modesty, they carelessly surrender their virginity to other men. Far from finding anything shameful in all this, they feel insulted if anyone refuses the favours they offer.

Diodorus Siculus (1st century BC)
World History, V.32

Strange customs

Diodorus Siculus gives the following colourful account of the Balearic islanders, another warrior people with whom the Celts were often associated as mercenaries in Mediterranean armies.

At wedding feasts relatives and friends take it in turn to lie with the bride in order of age from eldest downwards, first to last. The bridegroom is the last to receive this honour. Their funeral rites are also conducted in a singular way: they break up the corpse's limbs with wooden implements and put it into a vat that they then cover with a heap of stones. Their weapons consist of three slings: one that they carry around their heads, another around their waist and a third in their hands. In battle they can sling larger stones than anyone else, and with such force that they seem to have been shot by catapult. During assaults on strongholds they hit and disable defenders on the battlements, and in pitched battle they puncture shields, helmets and all the enemy's defensive armour. And they aim so accurately that they very seldom miss their target. This is because they start practising from early childhood, when even their

mothers force boys into constant use of the sling. They put some bread on a post as their goal, and the children go hungry until they hit the bread and get their mother's permission to eat it.

Diodorus Siculus (1st century BC)
World History, V.18

Feasts and lavish outlay

Posidonius, the first Greek writer to visit the interior of Gaul, continued Polybius' Histories. His book XXIII contained an interesting ethnographic study of the Celts.

Sometimes the Celts fight duals during their feasts. Though they are always armed at these gatherings, they engage in mock combat and spar among themselves with fists; they still sometimes end up with wounds, and then, becoming angry, if bystanders do not separate them, they go on to get killed.... In former times, when the hind quarters were served, the bravest man claimed the best cut, and if someone else wanted it, the two contestants stood up and fought to the death....

When many people dine together they sit in a circle, with the most important man in the central place, like the leader in a chorus; this is someone who excels the others by virtue of his martial skill, birth or wealth. Next to him sits the host, and then alternately on either side come all the others, in order of rank. Their shield-bearers stand behind them and the spearsmen sit in front in a circle like their lords, and feast in common in the same way. The servants take the drink around in ceramic or silver vessels that look like spouted cups; the dishes on which the food is arranged are made of the same materials or sometimes of bronze or are wooden or wicker baskets. The drink served to the rich is wine imported from Italy or Massaliote territory: they drink it neat or sometimes mixed with a little water; the less well-off drink a wheaten beer brewed with honey; the common people drink it plain, and it is called 'korma'. They drink from the same cup ... but they do so frequently.

Posidonius (135–51 BC)
Histories, XXIII (in Athenaeus, *Deipnosophists*, IV.40, IV.36)

The Celtic heroic tradition

The heroic ethos of the Celts, as of many other peoples, is neatly epitomized in the words of the Irish hero Cú Chulainn: 'Provided I am famous, I do not care whether I live but a single day in this world.' In such a society, in which life – and individual status – was dominated by an extremely sensitive regard for personal honour, it was essential that one should earn the respect of one's peers and, especially, of those poets, seers and learned men whose responsibility it was to shape and to interpret the mythology, the laws and the historical traditions of the tribal community....

Proinsias MacCana
'Celtic Heroic Tradition' in *The Celts*,
ed. by Kruta, Frey, Raftery, Szabó, 1991

To be a warrior among warriors was the ideal life for the Celt, but to die in a fight surrounded by friends, poets and a hundred dead enemies was the supreme consummation.... The preparation for the supreme moment, from his initiation onwards, gave the Celtic warrior his fearlessness and pride. Such qualities were noticed and commented upon by all the classical Greek and

This iron firedog and frame, possibly used for holding wine amphorae, was found in a grave with other provisions for feasting.

Roman writers, who also refer to the Celts' love of fighting and easy attitude to death. In the Cú Chulainn story, the sun god materializes to take over the functions of the warrior, who by dying for three days can remain mortal. In this bardo state he can ascend the three mystical worlds of the Celtic after-life: from earth-body to the physical spirit and finally into the radiant soul-light in which the sun himself is manifest. When Cú Chulainn sleeps he becomes joined to his own embodied radiance, inhabiting all worlds at once. This easy movement between the human warrior hero and his otherworldly archetype, the sun god, is a common practice in every kind of Celtic story. This is the key to the Celtic Mysteries – the merging of the spiritual, physical and imaginative planes.

John Sharkey
Celtic Mysteries: The Ancient Religion
1975

Languages and writing in Celtic culture

There is not one but several Celtic languages, and all belong to the Indo-European group. None, however, seems to have had the use of its own alphabet. Celtic inscriptions used borrowed alphabets that the Celts adapted. We have medieval Irish monks to thank for the preservation of some Insular Celtic literature, passed on to them by oral tradition.

Language as social evidence

The next point to be clarified is how it can be shown that the Celts of antiquity actually spoke tongues related to the surviving languages that in philological terminology are described as Celtic. This can be most readily demonstrated through the classics in the names of chieftains and tribes, and particular words or terms recorded as belonging to the Celts. This body of linguistic material falls within the Celtic branch of the Indo-European language family, and in many cases the anciently recorded words can be shown to have survived into the medieval and modern languages of the Celtic group.

There are three other primary sources on the language of the ancient Celts. In the first place there is the existence of a large number of inscriptions incorporating Celtic words and names, but mainly written in Latin, or more rarely in Greek. These were inscribed on altars and other monuments in the Celtic regions incorporated within the Roman Empire, and they have been found from as far apart as Hadrian's Wall and Asia Minor, Portugal and Hungary. The second source is akin. It is numismatic, but much more restricted in space. It is particularly valuable on account of coins inscribed with names, linguistically Celtic, that can be shown on archaeological and historical grounds to have been issued by Celtic kings or tribes. The third line of evidence has to do with place-names. These are as often river or other topographical names as those of actual settlements or strongholds. A direct link can be established in many cases through the classics in reference to the Celts, but the distributional evidence of Celtic place-names in Western and Central Europe conforms closely with the regions in which the Celts are known to have been strongest, and in which their influence lasted longest.

T. G. E. Powell
The Celts, 1983

The diversity of Celtic languages mirrors the different groups of Celts

The languages spoken by Celtic peoples today belong to two groups: Brythonic (or P-Celtic) and Goidelic (or Q-Celtic).... The Goidelic dialects include Irish, Gaelic (spoken in the west coasts of Scotland) and Manx; while Welsh, Cornish and Breton belong to the Brythonic branch. This distribution is the result of the migrations of the 5th and 6th centuries AD.... The migration of the Irish westward introduced the Goidelic dialect into the western parts of Scotland, where it became known as Gaelic, and into the Isle of Man; while Brythonic remained in use in Wales and Cornwall and was carried to Brittany by the folk movements from Devon and Cornwall in the 5th and 6th centuries.

The Irish form of Celtic remained dominant in Ireland ... until the 16th century, when English began to take over. But in Scotland the Celtic language had begun to be replaced by English somewhat earlier. In the Isle of Man, Manx was spoken extensively in the 17th century but has died out, apart from its use on ceremonial occasions. In Cornwall, too, Celtic

expired in the 18th century, but in Brittany it has remained. Today about half of the population can speak Breton. Celtic can be heard widely throughout western Ireland though hardly at all in Ulster, while in Scotland only fifteen per cent of the population are Gaelic speaking, but they are concentrated in the Hebrides. In Wales, however, twenty-six per cent of the population speak Welsh.

Barry Cunliffe
The Celtic World, 1992

The message carried by the language

The Celts of the extreme West – Bretons, Scots, Welsh and Irish – are today the sole guardians of the memory of the ancient Celtic peoples.... It is they who have preserved the legacy of an original literature, the work of

The number and position of lines carved on either side of the edge allow characters in ogham script to be identified on stones. On the page opposite is the Castlekeeran stone (Ireland).

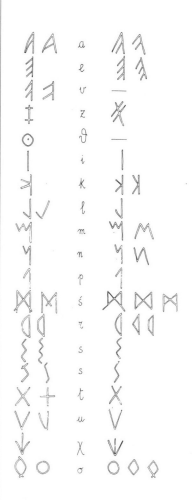

Celtic incriptions in the Lepontic alphabet appeared very early in northern Italy. Above: the alphabet used in the 6th century BC. Right: that of the 2nd and 1st centuries BC.

generations of anonymous poets, already several centuries old when it was written down by Irish monks in the early Middle Ages. The Insular Celts, last bearers of an oral tradition that, in other lands with a Celtic past, dispersed into the luxuriant world of folk legend, have kept alive a representational tradition that is as important as epic and mythological tales in the cultural treasure left to us by the peoples of ancient Europe....

Increasing weight is given today to one particular category of archaeological evidence: the texts, unfortunately short and very few, that the ancient Celts wrote in their own language with the help of various alphabets borrowed from the Mediterranean world....

The Celts emerge around the end of the 4th century BC from the anonymity of the ancient European peoples who had no writing. Their linguistic family, which had split off from early Indo-European nearly two millennia

A bove: 2nd- or 1st-century BC stone slab with Gallo-Greek inscriptions from Vaison-la-Romaine (Vaucluse).
Below: Iberian inscription from Contrebia (Spain).

previously, had a long history behind it at this time and was divided into several distinct groups that occupied vast areas of western central Europe....

However, analysis of so-called Lepontic inscriptions, composed at the end of the 6th century BC in characters derived from the Etruscan alphabet, indicate that Celtic groups, the first to make use of writing to record their language, were already well integrated into northern Italy – in present-day Lombardy and perhaps further south – when their Transalpine cousins came to settle in the Po valley and descended upon Rome.

Venceslas Kruta
Les Celtes en occident, 1955

Were the Celts bloodthirsty warriors?

Ancient authors stressed the courage and cruelty of the Celts, thereby paying tribute to the brave warriors who dared to confront them. These fierce, half-naked combatants were at a clear disadvantage against the Romans because of their equipment and their lack of organization.

Fearless combatants

All the Galatae [Celts], the Triballi [Thracians], and many other barbarians believe in the soul's immortality, so they have no fear of death and go out to embrace danger.

Iamblichus (AD 250–*c*. 330)
Life of Pythagoras, XXX.173

The Celts changed the conventional methods of warfare of the first millennium BC with their large iron hacking swords, their spear-throwing from fast two-horsed chariots, and their use of screaming naked riders to create terror and confusion.

John Sharkey
Celtic Mysteries: The Ancient Religion, 1975

Head hunters

Diodorus Siculus here alludes to a Celtic practice whose historical reality has never been absolutely proven.

When [the Celts] kill enemies in battle they cut off their heads and attach them to the necks of their horses. They leave the other bloody remains to their servants to carry off as plunder, and sing hymns of praise and victory songs, and finally nail these first-fruits to their houses, as people do with wild animals after certain kinds of hunting. They soak the heads of their most illustrious enemies in cedar oil and keep them carefully in a chest and show them off to strangers, each priding himself that for one or

Helmet from Casino Pallavicino, Italy (left). Pictish warrior (opposite) holding the head of an enemy.

other of these heads either a forebear, or his father, or he himself had refused to take a large sum of money. Some are said to boast that they have even refused its weight in gold for one of these heads, thereby displaying a barbaric sort of magnanimity, for there is nothing noble in refusing to sell the proofs of one's valour.

Diodorus Siculus (1st century BC)
World History, V.29

The terrible carnage at Telamon: fearsome but defeated Gauls

In 225 BC a coalition of Cisalpine Gauls, reinforced by Transalpine mercenaries, the Gaesatae, met the forces of Rome in a decisive battle at Telamon, on the coast of northern Etruria. Polybius describes it, probably following Fabius Pictor's eyewitness account.

The Insubres and Boii entered battle wearing breeches and with light cloaks wrapped around them, but the Gaesatae, in their presumptious self-assurance, had thrown off their clothes and took up position in the first rank, naked apart from their weapons, thinking they would fight better that way.... The first engagement took place on the hill.... Cavalry from both armies milled around....

Then, when the infantry troops made contact, there was a unique and extraordinary encounter.... A din arose from countless horns and war-trumpets, and such a loud clamour of war-cries broke from the whole army in concert that not only the trumpets and soldiers but even the surrounding countryside itself reverberated with echoes and seemed to be giving voice. Terrifying, too, were the appearance and movements of the powerful naked

men at the front, all in the prime of life. The men in the front lines were decked out with collars and bracelets of gold. The Romans then had a double incentive to fight, on the one hand horrified by what they saw before them, but also eager to win spoils.

When the [Roman] soldiers.... unleashed a dense shower of javelins upon them, their cloaks and breeches provided very useful protection for the Gauls in the rear, but for the naked men in front things turned out very differently from what they had expected, causing them much confusion and suffering. For the Gaulish shield is unable to cover the whole body, so the more naked they were and the larger their bodies were, the easier the javelins found it to hit their uncovered parts. Finally, unable to counterattack their assailants because of the distance between them and the rain of javelins, badly battered and sorely tried by the situation, some perished by launching themselves blindly upon their enemies in a fit of mindless rage and thereby going to a deliberate death, while others disorganized the ranks behind them by retreating backwards step by step and letting them see their terror. In this way the pride of the Gaesatae was broken under the impact of the javelins, but once the Romans had opened their ranks to withdraw their marksmen and instead launched their maniples against [the Gauls], the mass of the Insubres, Boii and Taurisci rushed headlong into the enemy and engaged in a violent hand-to-hand battle. Riddled though they were with wounds, they kept up equal spirits with the Romans but were collectively and individually disadvantaged by one thing – the nature of their equipment. Their shields gave far inferior protection, while their swords were far less effective in attack, since the Gaulish sword can only slash. When the Roman cavalry descended from the heights and charged vigorously from the flank the Celtic infantry was cut to pieces where it stood and the cavalry took flight.

Polybius (200–120 BC)
Histories, II.28–30

Chariot tactics

The lightly built Celtic war chariots combined speed and manoeuvrability. Their onslaughts were dreaded.

This is what [British] chariot warfare is like. First of all they drive about in

every direction hurling their javelins: the fear engendered by the horses and the din of the wheels is usually enough to disorder the enemy ranks. Then they slip between the squadrons of cavalry and leap off their chariots to fight on foot. Meanwhile the chariot drivers gradually withdraw from the battle and position the chariots in such a way that if the fighting men are overwhelmed by enemy numbers they can quickly return to them. They therefore combine the mobility of cavalry with the solidity of infantry in battle, and [the Britons] become so skilled in their use through training and daily practice that they can even control galloping horses on steep and dangerous inclines, make them slow down very quickly, and turn them around; they themselves can also dart out forwards along the shaft, stand steady on the yoke, and then return in a flash back to their chariots.

Caesar (104?–44 BC)
Gallic War, IV.33

The initial purpose of the chariot warrior was to drive furiously towards and along the front of the enemy ranks

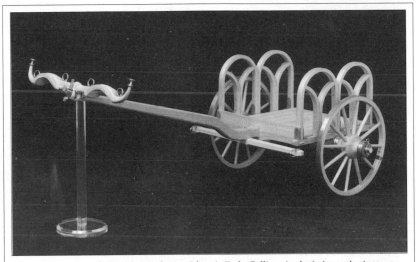

A reconstruction of a British war chariot (above). Early Gallic coin depicting a chariot scene (opposite). Gallic horseman and decorated sword found at Tesson (overleaf).

to instil terror by sight, and by the delivery of missiles, no less than by the tremendous noise that was kept up by shouting, horn blowing, and beating on the sides of the waggons drawn up to the flanks or in the rear. The warriors then descended from their chariots, which the charioteer held in readiness for a quick retreat if need be, while the warrior, with casting spear, or drawn sword, stood out to deliver a challenge to an opposing champion. The challenge was evidently in a set formula of boasts of prowess, and perhaps of lineage, incorporated in a war song. Indeed, a kind of frenzy was probably worked up. In inter-tribal fighting, it would appear that the main body of troops became involved only after this phase of individual contest, and perhaps only if one side had become certain of success in a general mêlée. The course of events against Roman armies must have involved the whole body of fighting men more directly, and it led to considerable modifications in battle order.

T. G. E. Powell
The Celts, 1983

Celtic warriors on horseback

At the time of the Roman conquest the Gauls preferred cavalry battles to other types of warfare. But these were not the tactics they used in earlier times.

Like the Greeks and Latins, the Celts and Belgae embarked upon the art of war with chariot combat. Contact with Mediterranean armies led the Italian and eastern Celts to give up this old practice. It disappeared more slowly from Gaul and Britain, where some peoples doggedly preserved their ancestors' ancient weapon.... In Celtica proper, territory of the Arverni and

Aedui, by the end of the 2nd century BC the war chariot had been reduced to no more than ceremonial use, a vehicle for processions or triumphs, as it had become and was to remain in republican Rome. Among the Belgae, by contrast, who had coalesced more recently and lived further away from civilized armies, it was regularly used as a fighting vehicle for a longer period, and there were some Belgic peoples, perhaps including the Remi, who stuck to it as though it were a defining feature of their identity.... Besides, it was not a bad way to fight: chariots carried a driver and a soldier on two wheels. Being very light, they reached the enemy quickly: standing upright, with the advantage of extra height, and close enough not to miss his target, the warrior would throw his lance or javelin and then withdraw at speed, or, if he preferred, get down to use his sword....

But noble Gauls in Caesar's time preferred to fight on horseback. There had doubtless once been a time when a horse served a warrior not primarily as a mount but as a vehicle, by which I mean that it afforded a way of reaching the battlefield more quickly, where the rider then fought on foot: horse-riding did no more than simplify the role of the war chariot. However, the war-horse was by now a fighting instrument, if I may so describe it. The terms 'cavalry' and 'aristocracy', 'horseman' and 'noble' became if not synonymous, at least inseparable....

All other weapons, especially in Celtic environments, seem to have been subordinate to the noble weapon, the sword, the weapon of close contact: just as, of all martial displays cavalry processions were preferred. The true

Celtic warrior was therefore a horseman of battles and skirmishes, charging and slashing.

Camille Jullian
Histoire de la Gaule, 1920

Celtic swords: long, but heavy and cumbersome

For attacking, the Gauls discovered the most suitable weapon for horsemen or tall foot-soldiers: a blunt-ended long iron sword, wide, flat, tapering and double-edged, which allowed a strong arm swinging it from high on horseback to slash into or fell an adversary's body. The Celts were attached to these weapons; they forged

enormous numbers of them for their multitudes, and it was probably because of them that they so often settled in iron-bearing areas of Europe and became the main agents for spreading the new metal at the expense of bronze. The large sword may have ensured them victory over various Ligurian or Illyrian populations of central Gaul, still with little experience of contact weapons; its cutting strength must have been largely responsible for the initial agitation of the southern world, which was only familiar with short, stabbing swords. A true cavalry sabre, the Celtic weapon seems to have had the double advantage of keeping the enemy at a distance while also reaching them.

But the Gauls' adversaries quickly discovered the shortcomings of this formidable instrument. To counter its dangerous edge the Romans reinforced the armour-plating of their shields and helmets, and the Gaulish sword, soft and poorly tempered, bent with the first blows. It could not thrust: to disarm it, Latin soldiers had only to be armed with long spears. Heavy and cumbersome, it was difficult for an arm to wield it fast and accurately.... It was a very easy matter for a forewarned adversary to avoid such blows; the barbarian's weapon then fell into thin air and he himself was left shaken and demoralized by the futile effort he had made, unable to respond to a reasonably active counter-attack. These swords resembled their masters: like them, they were made for display and were doomed to crumple.

Camille Jullian
Histoire de la Gaule, 1920

The manufacture of blades

Yet ... it seems possible that some of the [swords] may ... represent a regional style of manufacture, rather than the result of complex trading patterns, pilgrims depositing objects from far afield, travelling smiths or locally based craftsmen trained elsewhere, or any combination of these possibilities.

What is certain is that there were several major innovative centres of the ironsmiths' art in eastern Europe, particularly in Hungary. But both to east and west of this region there were other local workshops and artistic variants of the armourers' art, sharing certain motifs such as the dragon pair, the birds' heads and vegetal patterns. These frequently have distributions well beyond their original area of development, though this may be due not so much to trade alone as to the constant journeyings of professional warriors and even craftsmen.

Ruth and Vincent Megaw
Celtic Art: From its Beginnings to the Book of Kells, 1989

The druids

Men of the oaks, the druids were at the apex of a religious hierarchy that included soothsayers and bards. After a long and strict initiation they joined an élite that held power and knowledge. Their concerns were theology, morals and legislation as well as astronomy or divination.

A spiritual identity

Given the diversity and frequent inadequacies of our sources it would be unrealistic to expect from them a clear image of a unified, consistent order of religious belief. Nowhere have we the integral tradition as it might have been transmitted and interpreted by the druids and their associates in an independent Celtic society. No source or group of extant sources was designed to furnish an ordered, comprehensive picture of native religion as seen from within its own cultural community. The effect of this has been to accentuate the heterogeneity of Celtic religion, and it has sometimes led scholars to exaggerate its local and tribal character and to ignore the many features which reflect the underlying

unity of Celtic myth and ritual.... There were in fact individual gods whose cults extended over all, or over large parts of, the Celtic areas of Europe. 'Mercury', the most widely venerated of the Gaulish gods according to Caesar, is a case in point.

Proinsias MacCana
'Celtic Religion and Mythology' in *The Celts*, edited by V. Kruta, O. H. Frey, B. Raftery and M. Szabó, 1991

The idea that the ancient Celts had a common religion is based on comparative inferences from the corpus of records on Indo-European religions in our possession, and on iconographic studies made on La Tène art. It is actually impossible to establish any relationship, other than speculative, between these two sets of documentation. Furthermore, the same difficulties are encountered when attempting to draw parallels between the portraits of Gallo-Roman deities and those presumed to be from the La Tène pantheon. The reason for these difficulties probably lies in the basic incompatibility of the two systems of figurative expression.

Unlike most ancient religions, Celtic religion cannot have comprised a consistent and unchanging set of beliefs. It must have been a composite pantheon of tribal gods, local deities (often pre-Celtic), and cults pertaining to specific social classes, all bundled together in a flexible system organized around a handful of major pan-Celtic gods from a common mythological 'pool'. Something of this pool has filtered down through medieval Irish and Gaulish literature, precious vestiges of an oral tradition which continues to thrive on the islands, a tradition that

the advent of Christianity freed from the prohibition of written records.

Venceslas Kruta
'Celtic Religion' in *The Celts*, edited by V. Kruta, O. H. Frey, B. Raftery and M. Szabó, 1991

The origins of the word druid

The word druid as used in modern European languages is derived from continental Celtic through Greek and Latin texts. Caesar for instance writes of *druides*, and Cicero of *druidae*. These, of course, are Latinized forms in the plural. In the surviving Insular Celtic languages, *druí* (sing.), *druad* (plur.) are forms of the same word from Old Irish texts. *Dryw* is the Welsh equivalent in the singular. Druid, as a word, is considered to derive from roots meaning 'knowledge of the oak', or possibly 'great, or deep, knowledge'. Pliny compared the word to the Greek one for an oak tree, and seems to imply that its connection with oak was intended. The connection between the druids and the oak is indeed explicit in Pliny's account of the cutting of mistletoe from an oak tree by the druids, and the accompanying sacrifice of bulls. It is unfortunately unknown if this rite was connected with a tribal festival and for what purpose it was carried out. The oak groves at Olympia may also have been in Pliny's mind, and these certainly appear to have been a surviving Indo-European element in Greek cult comparable to the Celtic sacred woods, more particularly with the oak sanctuary (*Drunemeton*) of the Galatians. If the oak, principally but not exclusively amongst trees, was the symbol of deity, 'knowledge of the oak' would be apposite for those who mediated with the supernatural.

T. G. E. Powell
The Celts, 1983

On mistletoe

We must not forget the high regard in which the Gauls hold this plant. The druids (which is what they call their magicians) consider nothing more sacred than mistletoe and the tree that it grows on, so long as it is an oak. They select oak groves for the sake of that tree and will not perform any religious ceremony without its leaves. In fact the name 'druid' can even be derived from the word 'oak' if one employs a Greek etymology [*drys*, oak]. They think that anything that grows on an oak has been sent from heaven, and treat it as a sign that the god himself has chosen that tree. Mistletoe is actually very rare on oak trees, and when it is found, it is culled with great ceremony. In the first place, the collection must take place on the sixth day of the moon. This day is the beginning of their months, their years and their centuries (the latter last thirty years), and is a day on which the moon is already at full strength but is not yet in mid course. They give mistletoe a name that means cure-all.... Below the tree they prepare a sacrifice and religious feast, and bring two white bulls whose horns are bound for the first time. A priest clad in white climbs the tree, cuts the mistletoe with a golden hook and catches it on a white cloak. Victims are sacrificed with prayers to the god to render this offering propitious to the people who are making

it. They believe that mistletoe in a drink confers fertility upon any sterile animal and is an antidote to all poisons. Such superstitious faith do people generally place in frivolous objects.

Pliny the Elder (AD 23–79)
Natural History, XVI.95

Mystery, doctrine and priesthood

The druid was shaman, priest, poet, philosopher, physician, judge and prophet. His initiation included several intermediate stages. Thus, the course of study for an Irish bard or *fili* included verse forms, composition and recitation of tales, the study of grammar, ogham, philosophy and law. The next seven years were for more specialist studies

and included the secret language of the poets as the *fili* became an *ollamh*. He could then acquire the knowledge of genealogy, and the committal of events and laws into poetic forms to become a doctor of law. Finally the 'man of learning' would be fit to study incantations, divination and magical practice. 'Thus every druid a bard, though every bard did not aspire to be a druid.'

Caesar, describing the priesthood of Gaul, divides them into three groups: 'The vates practised soothsaying and studied natural philosophy. The bards celebrated the brave deeds of their gods in verse. The druids were concerned with divine worship, the due performance of sacrifices, both private and public, and the interpretation of ritual questions.' Their power seemed to be absolute, for in his observations the hardest penalty that could be levied on a person or family was exclusion from the sacrifices.

John Sharkey
Celtic Mysteries: The Ancient Religion
1975

The role of the druids

Within the larger Celtic community of Western Europe (never more than a patchwork of loose confederations), the druids were the custodians of vision and prophecy, sacrifice, poetic lore, the ritual calendar and the law   all the elements which united the different groups. The ritual traditions they maintained were oral ones.

John Sharkey
Celtic Mysteries: The Ancient Religion
1975

In the classical sources in the Posidonian group, on which we may place most reliance, the druids appear to have three main functions. In the first place they are the repositories of the traditional lore and knowledge of the tribe, whether of the gods, the cosmos and the other-world, or of the corpus of customary law and such practical skills as calendrical expertise. This body of knowledge was preserved in oral tradition (and probably mainly in verse form for mnemonic reasons) and continuity achieved by explicit instruction to the younger generation entering the priesthood. The druids' second function in Gaul was the practical application of their learning in law and to the administration of justice, though how this power operated side-by-side with that of the tribal chief or intertwined plants, while the male figure was all but ignored.... Plants had an almost religious importance in everyday life, and each year the druids gathered mistletoe, a solemn event that the Gauls took very seriously. Thus, the main features of Celtic art were closely tied to the most ancient forms of Celtic paganism, and were repeated with increasing frequency in the course of the half-millennium before Christ.

Paul-Marie Duval
'Celtic Art' in *The Celts*, edited by V. Kruta, O. H. Frey, B. Raftery and M. Szabó, 1991

Traditions of Celtic art

In essence, there are three rather than two 'traditions' of Celtic art. The first, continental La Tène art, started in the 5th century BC and continued until around the time of Caesar's conquest of Gaul in the 1st century BC. This art drew on native, classical and oriental sources (the last possibly derived second-hand from the Mediterranean) to produce a diversity of distinct but related styles. Although there is a certain amount of sculpture in stone and wood, most of the La Tène continental art that has come down to us was fashioned in metal, using a variety of techniques. Commonest is casting, but this can be combined with engraving, punching, tracing and scorping (grooving the metal with an implement known as a 'scorper'). Compasses were on occasion used in laying out designs. Bronze was the commonest metal employed, but gold, silver and even iron was on occasion ornamented. Coral or glass were sometimes used to enhance the natural surface of the metal. Ground was sometimes cut away to form openwork.

This sheet-bronze stylized horse's head was found in the Stanwick (Yorkshire) hoard with other chariot and horse trappings.

The second tradition is in some measure dependent on and derivative of the first, and comprises the La Tène art produced in Britain and Ireland from the 5th or 4th century BC until the Roman conquest by Claudius in AD 43 (or somewhat later in areas outside Roman control). Many of the elements of this 'Insular' La Tène art are shared in common with the continent, but the creations are mostly distinctive and represent regional styles of the La Tène tradition. The materials and substances employed are much the same, but British craftsmen showed a particular liking for basket patterns for infilling ground, and for enamelwork.

The third tradition of Celtic art is

that which flourished in Ireland and to a lesser extent Britain between the 5th and 12th centuries AD. This art borrows heavily from Roman motifs and it is a debated point as to what extent it owes a debt to La Tène art at all. From modest beginnings in later Roman Britain it was transmitted to Ireland in the 5th century and from the 6th flourished on Irish soil. Except by the Picts and Scots of northern Scotland, little Celtic art of note seems to have been produced in Britain after the 7th century. Of this 'Dark Age' Celtic art, most that has survived is in metal and stone, though a few rare pieces of woodwork show that this too was ornamented. A new medium however came to the fore – the illuminated manuscript. The range of ornamental techniques of the Iron Age artist was greatly extended by his post-Roman counterpart: gold filigree and granular work and the technique of cloisonné inlaying were developed in response to similar techniques employed by contemporary Germanic artists, while die-stamped foils and new materials such as niello (a black silver sulphide paste) were added to the repertoire.

The Norman penetration of Celtic Britain and Ireland seems to have led to the disappearance of Celtic art in the 13th century. Although elements of a Celtic tradition can be detected from time to time thereafter, it was not until the conscious revival of Celtic art in the 19th century that it became popular again. The factors behind its revival, particularly in Ireland, were originally partly at least political, but it rapidly appealed as an ornamental form to those who had little or no concern for issues of nationalism, and to judge by the proliferation of objects decorated in Celtic style, it has not yet outlived its vogue.

Lloyd and Jennifer Laing
Art of the Celts, 1992

This 1st-century gold torque comes from Snettisham, Norfolk, an area known as the territory of the Iceni, whose queen was Boudicca.

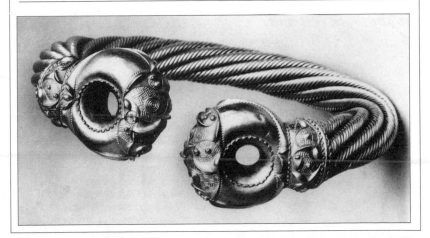

The first British heroine

Our only sources for the story of the Celts' resistance to Rome are Roman historians, but even they are obliged to concede the heroism of leaders such as Vercingetorix in Gaul and Caractacus in Britain. No figure seizes the imagination so much as the warrior queen Boudicca, who took over the rule of the Iceni, a tribe in Norfolk, and led a rebellion in AD 61 that cost Rome its chief town in the south east and thousands of British lives.

The rebellion against the Romans

Suetonius ... received tidings of the sudden revolt of the province. Prasutagus, king of the Iceni, famed for his long prosperity, had made the emperor his heir along with his two daughters, under the impression that this token of submission would put his kingdom and his house out of the reach of wrong. But the reverse was the result, so much so that his kingdom was plundered by centurions, his house by slaves, as if they were the spoils of war. First, Boudicca was scourged and his daughters outraged. All the chief men of the Iceni, as if Rome had received the whole country as a gift, were stript of their ancestral possessions, and the king's relatives were made slaves. Roused by these insults and the dread of worse, reduced as they now were into the condition of a province, they flew to arms....

Suetonius had the fourteenth legion with the veterans of the twentieth, and auxiliaries from the neighbourhood, to the number of about ten thousand armed men, when he prepared to break off delay and fight a battle.... On the other side, the army of the Britons ... was... so fierce in spirit that they actually brought with them, to witness the victory, their wives riding in wagons, which they had placed on the extreme border of the plain.

Boudicca, with her daughters before her in a chariot, went up to tribe after tribe, protesting that it was indeed usual for Britons to fight under the leadership of women. 'But now,' she said, 'it is not as a woman descended from noble ancestry, but as one of the people that I am avenging lost freedom, my scourged body, the outraged

chastity of my daughters. Roman lust has gone so far that not our very persons, nor even age or virginity, are left unpolluted. But heaven is on the side of a righteous vengeance; a legion which dared to fight has perished; the rest are hiding themselves in their camp, or are thinking anxiously of flight. They will not sustain even the din and the shout of so many thousands, much less our charge and our blows. If you weigh well the strength of the armies, and the causes of the war, you will see that in this battle you must conquer or die. This is a woman's resolve; as for men, they may live and be slaves.'

Nor was Suetonius silent.... He mingled encouragements and entreaties.... Suetonius gave the signal of battle. At first, the legion kept its position ... when they had exhausted their missiles, which they discharged with unerring aim on the closely approaching foe, they rushed out in a wedge-like column. Similar was the onset of the auxiliaries, while the cavalry with extended lances broke through all who offered a strong resistance. The rest turned their back in flight, and flight proved difficult, because the surrounding wagons had blocked retreat. Our soldiers spared not to slay even the women, while the very beasts of burden, transfixed by the missiles, swelled the piles of bodies. Great glory, equal to that of our old victories, was won on that day. Some ... say that there fell little less than eighty thousand of the Britons, with a loss to our soldiers of about four hundred, and only as many wounded. Boudicca put an end to her life by poison.

The Annals of Tacitus, XIV.31–7
Translated by Alfred J. Church and
William J. Brodribb, 1876

INDEX

Figures in italics refer to pages on which illustrations/captions appear.

ACKNOWLEDGMENTS

The author would like to thank Michel Comode, Dr Jörg Biel and the management of the Württembergisches Museum in Stuttgart. Grateful acknowledgment is made for permission to use material from the following work: (pp. 139–40 and 157–8) Stuart Piggott, *The Druids*, © 1968 and 1975 Stuart Piggott.

PHOTO CREDITS

Christiane Eluère
is Head Keeper of the French National Museums.
At the Musée des Antiquités Nationales,
St-Germain-en-Laye, she shares responsibility
for the protohistoric collections.
In 1987 she helped to organize the exhibition
'Treasures of the Celtic Princes'.
Her publications include *Les Ors préhistoriques* (1982),
L'Or des Celtes (1987) and
Secrets de l'or antique (1990).

© Gallimard 1992

English translation © Thames and Hudson Ltd,
London, and Harry N. Abrams, Inc., New York, 1993

Translated by Daphne Briggs

British Library Cataloguing-in-Publication Data

A catalogue record for this book is available from the
British Library

ISBN 0–500–300348

Printed and bound in Italy
by Editoriale Libraria, Trieste